The Twenty-Year Century

The Twenty-Year Century

*Essays on Economics
and Public Finance*

Felix G. Rohatyn

*Random House
New York*

Portions of this work have previously appeared in the following
publications: *The Economist,* the *New York Review of Books* and the *Wall
Street Journal.*

North American rights to pieces appearing in *The Economist* administered
by the New York *Times.*

Grateful acknowledgment is made to *Business Week* for permission to
reprint "A Plan for Stretching Out Global Debt." Reprinted from the
February 28, 1983, issue of *Business Week* by special permission, © 1983
by McGraw-Hill, Inc.

Library of Congress Cataloging in Publication Data

Rohatyn, Felix G., 1928–
The twenty-year century.

1. United States—Economic conditions—1981–
—Addresses, essays, lectures. 2. Economic history—
1971– —Addresses, essays, lectures. 3. Finance,
Public—United States—Addresses, essays, lectures.
4. Finance, Public—New York (N.Y.)—Addresses, essays,
lectures. I. Title.
HC106.8.R63   1983   330.973′0927   83-42908
ISBN 0-394-53450-6

Manufactured in the United States of America

98765432

FIRST EDITION

To my mother, who always deserved more credit

History proves that dictatorships do not grow out of strong and successful governments, but out of weak and helpless ones. If by democratic methods people get a government strong enough to protect them from fear and starvation, their democracy succeeds; but if they do not, they grow impatient. Therefore, the only sure bulwark of continuing liberty is a government strong enough to protect the interests of the people, and a people strong enough and well enough informed to maintain its sovereign control over its government.

—FRANKLIN D. ROOSEVELT

Acknowledgments

This book could never have come about without the constant encouragement, gentle needling and tireless editing of Jason Epstein at Random House. I must also express my thanks to those other editors who, over the last few years, taught me to write and gave generously of their own time and of the space of their publications to enable me to present my views. First among many is Bob Silvers of the *New York Review of Books*, who, time after time, helped me to turn speeches, testimony and other writings into articles for his publication. Lew Young of *Business Week*, Mike O'Neill and Jim Wieghart of the New York *Daily News*, Charlotte Curtis and Ed Klein of the New York *Times*, Meg Greenfield of the Washington *Post*, Bob Bartley of the *Wall Street Journal*, Andrew Knight of *The Economist* and many others made their op-ed pages and publications available as well as their counsel and advice. Without them I would still be writing accounting memos.

Contents

The Twenty-Year Century

Introduction

IN 1941 HENRY LUCE STATED THAT THE TWENTIETH
century would be known as the "American Century." The
"American Century" lasted only twenty years. From 1945 to
1965 the United States dominated the world: we were the ,
foremost military power, the industrial leader, the dominant
financial power. American nuclear weapons maintained a Pax
Americana; the dollar was the basis of the Bretton Woods
agreements, which sustained a flourishing world economy;
American cars, American refrigerators, American televisions
set the standards for the rest of the world. The philosophy of
the New Deal, that every American was entitled to
employment opportunity and a minimum level of security,
together with our military and economic dominance, reinforced
our conviction that a new day was dawning in both American
and world affairs. We Americans would eradicate poverty and
injustice at home, and then, with the benefit of our experience,
the world would follow our example. Sputnik, the Vietnam
war, Watergate, Japanese economic and technological
competition and two oil shocks helped bring the American
Century to an early end.

From 1965 to date, the American economy has oscillated
between growth with inflation, and recession combined with
unemployment. These oscillations have become steeper as
residual rates of inflation and unemployment have increased
from one cycle to the next.

While we blame the Vietnam war for much of the inflation
of the 1970s, our response to the 1973 and 1979 oil shocks

did its share of damage too. We paid for a tenfold increase in oil prices, largely with debt and inflation. So did the rest of the world: Third World and Eastern European debt has ballooned to about $700 billion.

In 1981 American inflation reached 14 percent, while the prime rate reached 20 percent and our national debt grew to over $1 trillion. In response the Reagan Administration slammed on the monetary brakes while cutting taxes and increasing defense outlays. The result was the steepest recession since World War II, 12 million workers unemployed, a skyrocketing dollar and world-wide economic contraction. Predictably, this recession reduced inflation significantly. The recession, along with conservation, brought oil prices down, while food prices fell because of large crops and favorable weather.

By the summer of 1982, the severity of the economic contraction, together with the huge sovereign debts accumulated in the last few years, brought the world banking system to the edge of financial catastrophe. First Mexico, then Brazil failed to meet debt commitments. Argentina's economy, as a result of the Falklands war, became shakier than ever. Those three countries owed an aggregate of almost $200 billion to Western banks and governments. The Federal Reserve (Fed) and the International Monetary Fund (IMF), together with the Western banks, led the rescue efforts that prevented massive defaults. At the same time the Fed reversed its tight money policies, lowered interest rates dramatically and embarked upon a significantly more stimulative monetary policy. The combination of easier money and lower interest rates, together with the stimulus provided by huge budgetary deficits, inevitably brought an economic upturn. This was further stimulated by lower oil prices as the Organization of Petroleum Exporting Countries (OPEC) came more and more under the pressure of reduced world-wide demand, and by a moderation of wage increases as unemployment remained high. Energy price increases shook the world's economy in the 1970s and swept away numbers of incumbent political leaders; the positive impact of falling energy prices should be correspondingly significant.

However, the recovery that began early in 1983 can easily abort unless there is significant new capital investment, if imports increase sharply at the expense of domestic production and unemployment remains high, and if the present imbalance between rich and poor, between America's Sunbelt and Frostbelt, between cities and suburbs, persists.

Whether the recovery is extended or brief, it is likely to be just one more in the series of oscillations to which our economy has recently been subjected unless we find some way to eliminate our underlying economic weakness. We will have blasted ourselves out of a self-induced recession by an enormous fiscal and monetary stimulus; but if nothing fundamental has changed, we will be on our way to the next inflation, the next downturn with higher unemployment, higher debts and more dislocation than other previous recoveries. It is as if we have begun to institutionalize the passage from crisis to crisis, have learned to accept these oscillations as if they were normal.

New York City in the period 1970–1975 was clearly headed toward disaster. The politicians had learned to paper over the city's budget deficits, but the reality could not be avoided forever. The city's short-term debt had grown from practically nothing to $6 billion in five years and more borrowings were needed constantly. When the bond markets rejected further New York City borrowing in mid-1975, an impromptu coalition of government, business and labor began the difficult process of bringing an annual operating deficit of $1.8 billion, together with short-term borrowings of $6 billion, down to zero. The process took five years and included the most arduous and painful control of spending in any modern city's experience, as well as various measures to stimulate growth. New York City balanced its budget in 1981 and 1982 and, as a result of significantly increased state aid together with stronger-than-expected economic growth, had a budget surplus in fiscal 1983. New York is now credit-worthy and in the strongest financial condition in a decade.

The city in 1983 overcame serious budgetary problems which were the result of the recession, the recent overvalued dollar which reduced tourism and foreign investment, and federal budget cutbacks. However, it is equally true that new labor contracts in 1982, excessive by any current standard, contributed much to the problem. It is unfortunately also true that the immediate political reaction was to suggest tax increases rather than to try to renegotiate parts of this contract. It is furthermore distressing to observe that city institutions specifically created to prevent a recurrence of past fiscal problems, such as the Emergency Financial Control Board, chose to look the other way. If New York's institutional memory can forget its traumatic brush with bankruptcy in only six years, what can we expect at the national or international levels, where printing money has always been a way out of an immediate problem?

The essays contained in this volume are much concerned with my experience during the New York City fiscal crisis of 1975 and thereafter. What we were able to do in New York, as well as what we failed to do, has greatly influenced my thinking on matters of public policy. Inevitably, the reader will find that I repeat certain themes and arguments from one essay to the next, as my concerns became building blocks for further argument in subsequent essays. These essays (except where noted) are in chronological order running from the most recent in August and September 1983 to the earliest in December 1978. Except for the elimination of the more obvious repetitions, they appear essentially in their original form.

Since these essays cover a period of nearly five years, the context in which they were written has to be considered, and I have attempted in each case to describe it in some detail. Suffice it to say here that some of these pieces were written in a period of high inflation, skyrocketing oil prices and the presidency of Jimmy Carter, while others were written in a period of steep recession, low inflation, strong recovery and the presidency of Ronald Reagan.

Oil prices and interest rates have come down much faster than I had anticipated. The depth and length of the world-wide recession that brought them down were also greater than I had expected, as was the strength of the recovery. The fundamental problems created by the world-wide shift in wealth, which OPEC created, have not gone away, however. The mountains of debt created to pay for oil are still there. A recovery limited to the United States will be insufficient to secure either the world or the United States itself from further trouble, while further deterioration here or abroad will bring unpredictable crises.

The years in which I wrote these essays were perplexing and turbulent. They witnessed increasing frustration among both voters and governments in the face of economic and social problems that were becoming more and more intractable. In the Western democracies this was reflected by increasingly rapid changes in governments, without any clear indication of philosophical preference. Conservative gains in the United Kingdom, Germany and the United States coincided with liberal and socialist gains in Canada, France, Sweden, Italy, Greece and Spain. As the world-wide economic crisis worsened, the only consistent note was a call for change. The performance of the communist countries was a disaster; so was that of much of the Third World.

It is because I am convinced that economies are fundamentally unpredictable and that we have gradually exhausted most of our margins of safety that I believe in the need for actions that affect trends instead of just numbers. What I call for in these essays are mechanisms that can negotiate balanced responses to systematic distortions so that we will not always have to bet on essentially unpredictable market reactions. Our biggest economic competitors, as well as our biggest customers, Western Europe and Japan, have such negotiating mechanisms in one form or another. In Japan, the Ministry of International Trade and Industry (MITI), together with a system of consultation and consensus among business, labor and government, responds to Japan's needs. In Europe, first the European Coal and Steel Authority and then the European Common Market grew out of the need for cooperation. Although business/labor relationships vary widely in Europe, both Germany and Japan have institutionalized the relationships and the negotiating cycle far beyond what is done here.

The responsibility of government is to act early, when the popular perception of need is only diffuse, at best. That is why it is important to anticipate and attempt to modify trends before they result in crises. The cumulative impact of early action can be extraordinarily great when it is maintained over a period of time. For instance, had the United States imposed a fifty-cent-per-gallon tax on gasoline in 1973 at the time of the first oil shock, the United States Treasury would by now have collected some $500 billion from the tax and our national debt would be half of what it has become. That reduction in debt would also have saved an additional $100 billion or so in interest costs, and would have reduced inflation accordingly. Such a tax would have driven the U.S. auto industry to build fuel-efficient cars early enough to have withstood the onslaught of foreign competition, with less resulting unemployment. It would have benefited the country as a whole and, by keeping our consumption down, would have kept world oil prices lower and benefited the rest of the world too. But such a tax was not to be. Band-Aids, deficits and inflation were politically easier.

OPEC's current weakness gives us a new opportunity to strike a blow for energy independence with the imposition of a crude oil import fee together with a gasoline tax. But as I write it appears that once again this opportunity will pass us by. The inevitable next convulsion in the Middle East, with possible supply interruption and price increases, will find us as naked as the last one.

Crises are not inevitable; but they become more likely in the absence of institutions that can anticipate and forestall them. Whether the next crisis will be financial, energy-based or food-based, military or social, no one can tell. But whatever it will be, we need responsible mechanisms for dealing with such crises, whether they are national or multinational. We must institutionalize ways to address those trends that are likely to cause crises, even if the resulting solutions are only temporary and partial, for this is probably the best we can do.

I am, by temperament, an active negotiator. Whether in connection with mergers or reorganizations of companies in difficulties, as chairman of a committee trying to avoid the bankruptcy of the New York Stock Exchange or as chairman of New York's Municipal Assistance Corporation, commonly called "MAC," which helped to prevent the bankruptcy of New York City, I have dealt with matters that have all had the following in common: they were finite, measurable and describable, and they all involved plans of financial reorganization calling for a balance of forces and an equitable distribution of interests. I had had, by and large, little or no responsibility for the past performance of the various organizations I was called upon to advise, and this gave me a degree of detachment in diagnosing their strengths and failings. Many of these situations involved matters of face as well as money, of actual power as well as prestige. Most of them had to be dealt with under considerable pressure of time and emotion, and with reasonable amounts of discretion. Discretion in the public sector is vastly different from discretion in the private sector, but some basic rules apply generally, including respect for an individual's confidences, the sanctity of one's word and the maintenance of consistent positions with all parties.

My experience has been with process and active negotiation rather than with theory and academic or other disengaged analysis. As an investment banker, I had tested the negotiating process in the private sector. I then had the opportunity in

1970–1972 to test it in a semipublic situation as chairman of the "Crisis Committee" of the New York Stock Exchange. It was a successful experiment, which, as with all successes, included a good bit of luck. A few years later the near bankruptcy of New York City gave me the opportunity to test the negotiating process entirely in the public sector.

In dealing with the New York City crisis and as chairman of MAC, I came in direct contact and had to contend with many of the institutions typical of those that move the country as a whole: banks, labor unions, city government with its mayors and city councils, a Democratic governor and a state legislature split between a Republican senate and a Democratic assembly. To obtain credit assistance from the federal government, we had to deal first with a Republican and then with a Democratic President, as well as with the relevant congressional committees representing the most diverse regional interests. We had to deal with the press and television, with subway riders whose fares were being raised, with City University students faced with tuition for the first time, and with taxpayers tempted to move to Arizona. We were attacked from the left for being heartless tools of the banks, and from the right for being soft on labor and naïve in our sympathy for the poor.

For someone like me, having come to America during the war and having spent my entire business career with one private banking house, the New York City affair was an extraordinary education. As chairman of the Municipal Assistance Corporation, I was soon called upon to speak publicly (a terrifying experience at first), to testify before government committees and finally to write. The writings in this volume are the result.

The reader will note several themes running through these reflections, all born of the New York experience. Though I believe the marketplace knows best most of the time, I am skeptical that it should always be the ultimate arbiter of economic action, and I am more than willing to interfere with it when it becomes a distorting rather than a benign influence. In 1975 the marketplace condemned New York City to bankruptcy. This would have been a needless catastrophe for the people who lived in the city, who worked for the city and who had invested in the city, to say nothing of the city's suppliers of goods and services. For all their ideology, some of America's most vociferous free-marketers cheered us on when we restructured the city's debt (with limited but critical federal assistance), froze wages, imposed a Financial Control Board and even resorted to a temporary moratorium on repayment of short-term debt to avoid bankruptcy. We do not live in a free-market economy, as witness OPEC, farm support prices and the influence of the Federal Reserve on interest rates; we live in a mixed economy and will do so for the foreseeable future.

I see no contradiction between the beliefs on the one hand that an activist government has an obligation to redress imbalances and provide for those who, through no fault of their own, are unable to provide for themselves, and on the other hand that we need to live within our means. I believe this country's budget must be in balance at full employment, by which I do not mean the current definition of "full employment" that contemplates 6 percent unemployment.

I strongly favor private employment, but I see no philosophical difference between a job created by a defense contractor working on a weapons system and a job created by an engineering company working on a publicly financed mass transit or sewer system. Today public works employment is derided as "dead-end" or a government dole. But how do these jobs differ in an economic or philosophical sense from jobs in defense? More mass transit and bridges might prove to be more desirable assets on the national ledger than more weapons.

High technology will put relentless downward pressure on employment in every sector of our economy, even the most rapidly growing ones. I believe that we must take vigorous action by way of education, training, stimulus of industry,

public works and private and public employment to reduce
unemployment significantly. While we move forward toward
this goal, deficits can be tolerated only as long as the trend
toward eventual balance is consistent and real. We cannot
tolerate, even in times of recession, deficits that will double our
national debt every five years, as is the case at present. Such
sacred budgetary cows as Social Security, Medicare, Medicaid
and federal and military pensions will, sooner or later, have to
be brought under control and their growth sharply restricted.
The Pentagon must sacrifice some large weapons systems and
replace them with greater conventional forces and a peacetime
draft. As the current recovery continues, new taxes are
inevitable.

Above all, our economy must grow. New York was saved
from bankruptcy, and its citizens accepted austerity, because
they believed there was hope for a better future. The fulfillment
of that hope required strong economic growth to limit the
suffering and eventually to balance our budget. For democracy
to survive, economic growth is a sine qua non.

The need for balance and a sense of fairness is also essential.
In the United States, regional balance is strained by the growth
of the Sunbelt at the expense of the Northeast and Midwest.
Industrial balance is affected by the simultaneous decline of our
basic industries and growth of the service sector. Current
budget and tax policies have increased the disparities between
rich and poor, and will increase them further. Those who need
education the most are likely to get the least; as population
and immigration increase, technology and foreign competition
will slow the creation of new American jobs.

Regional balance is in the long-term interest of the entire
country. President Reagan's New Federalism initiative was
flawed in many respects and is no longer on the political
agenda. Great benefit, however, could be achieved by a New
Federalism properly constructed. The reader will find
throughout most of these essays an attempt to search for
principles of regional balance and reallocation of federal-state

responsibilities. I recognize the political difficulties involved here, but I believe balance is more achievable today than it was ten years ago. There is practically no part of the United States today that believes itself to be immune from unemployment, poverty, the need for more services, the pressure of illegal immigration. The Sunbelt lies precariously between two regions in great difficulty: Mexico and the northern parts of the United States. It may no longer be able to absorb the immigration coming up from the south or down from the north. Perhaps a political accord could be negotiated so that instead of being a country of winners and losers, we can all benefit somewhat. It seems to me at least worth trying.

The need for balance is becoming more and more acute both in the United States and abroad. The role of government is to provide stabilizers when balance becomes precarious. Most of the time free markets will provide this balancing mechanism, but when markets become destabilizing, government must step in as the countervailing force. This can happen when foreign-exchange rates become distorted by such political considerations as capital transfers, sheer speculation and manipulation, as is currently the case in the yen/dollar relationship which greatly affects several of our industries. It can also happen when climate and natural resources greatly benefit one region at the expense of another, as in the case of the Sunbelt versus the Frostbelt. Regional and industrial balance, in some respects, go hand in hand. The hardest-hit areas of our country are tied to those industries in greatest difficulties.

In arguing for a restructuring of our basic industries, with government credit assistance through an organization like the Reconstruction Finance Corporation of the 1930s and 1940s, I am neither suggesting a bailout of inefficient firms nor being indifferent to investment in high technology. There is no contradiction between supporting high technology and having healthy, competitive automobile and metallurgical industries. Nor is there any reason that high-technology industries cannot be based in older industrial areas, as indeed they are in the areas around Boston. Some of the potentials of high technology can be exploited only by an overall upgrading of our basic manufacturing skills. Robots and sophisticated electronics are integral to the auto industry just as high-strength alloys and sophisticated avionics are a part of today's aircraft industry. The opportunities for high-technology development within our basic industries are obvious.

Market forces are destroying many of our basic industries, possibly permanently, but these market forces are by no means free. Currency fluctuations due to financial speculation affect trade and employment just as much as subsidies, hidden or open. So do the policies of European and Asian governments as well as of OPEC. I do not believe we ought to remain passive under these circumstances. We need a continuing institutionalized response.

In this book the reader will find arguments for a stabler international monetary system, one that would impose limits upon currency fluctuations. To avoid greater and greater levels of mindless protectionism, such a system should be coupled with a plan to restructure the world's ominous sovereign debt.

The advantages of free trade are obvious. The economic and social tragedy of unemployment is equally obvious. We now practice selective protectionism through mechanisms such as steel "trigger pricing" or "voluntary" auto restraint agreements with the Japanese. I do not quarrel with the need to provide temporary relief to one or another of our basic industries. But this relief should come as part of a plan to restructure the industry in need of protection to make it competitive, not simply to pass higher prices along to the American consumer. Such restructuring should include wage concessions, investment commitments and productivity improvements. The objective must be to provide the American consumer with a competitive product at a competitive price at the end of a limited period of protection.

To reconstruct America's basic industries and its

infrastructure will require, among other things, negotiation. I see a reconstituted Reconstruction Finance Corporation (RFC) helping to perform this role.

The last years of the twentieth century will probably witness an increasing capital shortage coupled with increasing demands for job security. The RFC that I envisage would be able to provide (or withhold) capital in exchange for concessions (from management, labor, banks, suppliers, local governments) leading to healthy industries, economical public works and greater job security.

Throughout these pages runs the idea of cooperation among business, labor and government, more or less formally instituted. This does not mean an unholy, statist alliance aimed at manipulating American citizens. What I have in mind are structures and forums within which these three important components of our society can negotiate matters of common interest. Before we argue about how to divide the pie, we must find a way to make the pie bigger. This cannot happen without an end to the wasteful antagonisms that divide business, labor and government. A revised RFC, new ways of approaching labor contracts, greater coordination among government agencies dealing with trade and the economy—all these should become subjects of examination.

I do not question the need to ensure attention to the public interest as part of such business/labor/government cooperation. Environmental protection, occupational safety, consumer protection, affirmative action and many similar concerns are part of the fabric of our society. Such protection must be maintained even though I and many of my colleagues in the business world tend to find the associated bureaucracy frustrating and costly. The current conservative drive to roll back many of these programs goes much too far and is not in the national interest. It will therefore fail sooner or later.

A reconstituted RFC would not function as an independent state, but as the financing and development arm of a tripartite board that would include public as well as government representatives. The policy recommendations of this board, when approved by the President, would then be executed by the RFC.

The reader will find in these essays no separate dissertation on taxes. I have consistently supported a significant increase in gasoline taxes to provide budget revenues, promote conservation, protect our auto industry's investment in fuel-efficiency and prepare for the next oil shock. I believe our failure to impose such a tax in 1973 was as serious an economic mistake as we have made since World War II. As for the arguments about consumption taxes versus income taxes, I am decidedly skeptical. Consumption taxes (sales taxes, VATs, etc.) strike me as essentially regressive, often penalizing those who can least afford them. Congress has recently legislated massive tax incentives aimed at encouraging savings and capital formation. It has practically eliminated the corporate income tax. Despite these incentives, high interest rates have inhibited both consumer demand and industrial investment. In taxes, as in everything else, I would encourage balance. Local taxes including sales taxes are already heavily weighted toward consumption. At the national level, a simplified income tax along the lines of the one proposed by Senator Bill Bradley of New Jersey and Representative Richard Gephardt of Missouri (but not a flat tax), a minimum corporate income tax and a gasoline tax would be my preferred mix. I do not like taxes, but I do not believe Americans are overtaxed; we need a different mix.

The reader will also find no separate dissertation on defense, only my repeated contention that we are spending too much on nuclear overkill and too little on conventional arms. I believe in the draft as a matter of fairness as well as of economy. I would rather that we deployed six more divisions in Europe than sixty Pershing missiles. When the reaction time to a possible missile attack is down to ten minutes, and the most important decision in the history of the world can be made by a computer to "launch on warning," the time has come to take greater risks for peace. I am for a strong defense, but the notion that nuclear war is "winnable" strikes me as utterly demented.

Underlying these writings is my conviction that if the various pieces of the puzzle can be made to fit, the result will be a satisfactory economy and a viable society. We are used to looking at things from the top down instead of from the bottom up. But endless arguments about the budget, macroeconomics, tax policy and so forth are no substitute for dealing with the actual pieces that make up the whole. The Greenspan Commission on Social Security was a welcome exception to our usual abstract approach to economic problems, and its example ought to be extended to other areas; education is a good example. We want to compete technologically with the Japanese, but our elementary and secondary schools largely ignore mathematics and science, while our universities turn out lawyers and MBAs instead of engineers and chemists. This is not a problem that will be solved by the market system alone; it requires government intervention to some extent.

If we have learned anything so far it is that no one person, no one political party, no one economic theory has the answer to these problems. Recent conservative experiments in the United Kingdom and the United States have been admired because of their apparent simplicity and intellectual toughness. They will ultimately fail not because of their ideological determination to reduce taxes and spending but because of their elemental insensitivity and unfairness, and their unwillingness to use government as a balancing mechanism. Past excesses cannot be redressed by increasing current imbalances.

At the other extreme, the socialist experiment in France is in deep trouble. Low productivity and crushing levels of taxation, together with overambitious social goals, have created serious and unnecessary difficulties for one of the wealthiest countries on earth.

Somewhere between those extremes there must be a better

approach, at once cooperative and pragmatic, an approach that
will deal piecemeal with issues too complicated to lend
themselves to sweeping solutions. Such an approach may
sometimes appear to be ambiguous compared to the hard and
simply defined edge of today's conservative ideologies, but
reality too is ambiguous, and the hard edges of today's
conservatism are more hard than truly conservative.

The basic issues for the future of the world are

- economic growth and job creation among Western industrial
  nations
- arms reduction agreements between East and West
- ample food, cheap energy, growing trade and debt
  rescheduling so that the Third World can also develop

The achievement of these goals requires the philosophical
predisposition as well as the leadership of the U.S. government.

In most parts of the world, the standard of living cannot
keep up with the birth rate. More and more people go hungry
while their governments squander their meager resources on
expensive weapons systems. We Americans limit the production
of our own foodstuffs and encourage the purchase of arms by
people who cannot afford them, in a senseless competition with
both our allies and our enemies. This is not a recipe for
stability.

The reader will find in these pages serious concern with the
strength of our banking system and the debt burden of the
Third World. The United States has become a major exporting
nation; so is Japan; so are the nations of Western Europe. The
Western economies are too mature to provide sufficient export
markets for each other. For strong recovery to occur among
the industrial nations, their Third World export markets must
be viable. This is not the case today, in large part because of
the Third World's debt burden. The United States must take
the lead in an effort to stabilize the world's monetary system
and to provide economic breathing room by restructuring
much of the Third World's debt. Economic growth for the

balance of the century will depend in no small part on the ability of India, China, Indonesia, Mexico, Brazil and Pakistan to finance Western-made goods for their large populations. If the mature Western democracies are to become the locomotives to move the rest of the world, the rest of the world has to cooperate, and long-term debt restructuring ought to be the first step. There is a real danger that the unintended result of certain of the IMF's current programs would be populist, anti-American governments emerging in Brazil, Argentina and other Latin American countries, ultimately including Mexico. That is not an acceptable risk.

This is also true insofar as our foreign policy objectives are concerned. It seems to me self-evident that the best counter to the threat of communism and radicalism in Central America is a healthy and growing Mexican economy rather than military aid to El Salvador.

To exercise leadership abroad, the United States must be secure at home. Technology transmits ideas and pictures more rapidly even than missiles transport their warheads. In our world-wide ideological competition with the Soviet Union, our ability to provide freedom, fairness and wealth to our people will have a far greater impact than will a new generation of weapons. There is no excuse for a nation as rich as ours to tolerate the squalor of our ghettos, the degradation of our schools, the decay of our cities, the plight of our farms, the decline of many of our industries, conditions that cannot be found in any other advanced Western industrial society. The improvements due to the current economic recovery will not go far enough to redress many of these conditions and will be uneven in their distribution.

Our growing problems are coupled with our growing inability to legislate fairly and sensibly because of the explosive intrusion of money into politics. Legislators, at both the local and national levels, are, most of the time, perfectly aware of what needs to be done, but it is often political suicide for them to do it. Television has made political advertising as well as political reporting into melodrama and clichés, expressing the superficial and the controversial, making the politician a prisoner of promises he cannot keep in exchange for popularity he cannot sustain. The result is government by crisis. We wait until things get so bad that everyone can share the blame and everyone can understand that there is no longer a way out. In New York City this led to the bankruptcy crisis of 1975, which we were able to overcome through courageous political leadership, business/labor cooperation, state and federal assistance and luck. It would be foolish to wait for a similar emergency to befall the entire country.

The reader will find no "new economic theory" in what follows. Many of these essays grew out of congressional testimony, each dealing with a specific problem: assistance to New York City; the Third World debt and the International Monetary Fund; the creation of a Regional Energy Development Corporation or a new Reconstruction Finance Corporation; the New Federalism and the states. They are a relatively modest series of suggestions, to some extent overlapping and inevitably somewhat repetitive, in an attempt to alter some trends that I find profoundly disturbing.

I have often been criticized for being overly pessimistic. In these essays the reader may find justification for this criticism. Many of my worst fears have not come about so far, and the current performance of our economy has been significantly better than I expected. However, I am professionally trained to assess risk and, possibly because of my background, to plan for the "worst case." I do not believe that I am seeing ghosts.

Nevertheless, I am convinced that we can deal with our problems; in fact, I believe that in dealing with them we shall find our greatest opportunities. We have enormous assets, a stable political system, a huge domestic market and a free, competitive, inventive society. We must make the most of them. However, we must be realistic about our problems and skeptical of miraculous "new" solutions. There are no technological breakthroughs in government or economics, and those who offer them should be treated with the greatest reserve. Identifying an appropriate role for government is a major unresolved question in the Western democracies. However, courage, common sense and cooperation consistently applied can work miracles. We saw that on a limited scale in New York City; I believe it is worth trying nationally.

Chapter One

THIS ESSAY WAS WRITTEN IN THE SPRING OF 1983, A time of strong economic recovery. It grew out of a commencement address I delivered at Fordham University and testimony to the Committee on Ways and Means of the U.S. House of Representatives.

It attempts to assess the economic recovery which was gaining strength at that time, as well as the broader domestic and international agenda that must still be addressed if the recovery is to be lasting.

In it the reader will find many themes taken up in earlier essays, which are now pulled together, I hope, into a coherent whole.

Following the essay are excerpts from testimony to the House Committee on Banking, Finance and Urban Affairs later in 1983, which will clarify some of the issues raised in the arguments about industrial policy. I have tried to define what "industrial policy" means to me, since opposition to the concept is based on totally different assumptions about its meaning and its substance.

Time
for a Change

THE ECONOMIC RECOVERY NOW UNDER WAY APPEARS TO have increasing strength and momentum. The stock market has moved up dramatically, interest rates have come down significantly, consumer spending is up, inflation is down, production is growing. That is welcome news to everyone. There are two possible explanations for this recovery. One is that supply-side economics works and that the Reagan tax and budget programs enacted in 1981, together with monetarism, are producing long-term economic growth with low inflation and high investment. The other is that we are experiencing a normal, or slightly subnormal, cyclical rebound after a steep recession, stimulated by consumer spending, high deficits and easy money—in short, a classical Keynesian recovery.

Of the two explanations, the second one appears to me closer to the mark. Last summer monetarism, coupled with the deficits created by the 1981 budget program, produced the steepest recession since World War II with the highest real interest and unemployment rates, and almost bankrupted the world. When some of our largest companies and credit institutions, followed by Mexico and Brazil, went to the edge of bankruptcy, the Federal Reserve reversed its tight money policy, lowered interest rates and increased the money supply significantly. This reversal, helped by last summer's tax package, permitted the present recovery to take hold. Inflation has been brought down dramatically by a worldwide contraction caused by economic austerity, by the creation of 35 million unemployed in the industrial world, by the sharp reduction in oil prices as a result of reduced consumption, and by lower food prices as a result of good harvests and good weather.

The boom in the stock market was set off by lower interest rates

driving funds from money-market accounts into equities, as well
as by huge inflows of foreign capital from investors who looked to
the dollar for political insurance and to our economy as the only
safe haven. It was at least partly this inflow of foreign capital that
permitted our deficit to be financed while a minimum of borrowers
were crowded out, and interest rates were significantly reduced.

Given the depth of the recession and the stimulus provided by
a $200 billion deficit and easier money, a recovery had to happen.
It is consumer-led, deficit-financed and classically Keynesian in
character. It is also pushed along by the stock market. The boom
in the market has increased market values by over $600 billion
during the past year. *Business Week* cites a rule of thumb that 6
percent of increased market values is translated into consumer
spending. This alone amounts to almost $40 billion. The stock
market boom has also brought with it vast speculative excesses
that make those of the 1960s look tame, and that should be viewed
with serious concern.

This is not to deny the real achievements of the Reagan Administration. By the end of the last Administration, we were
headed for an inflationary disaster. Partly as a result of its own
failures and partly as a result of forces beyond its control, the
Carter Administration left a legacy of double-digit inflation, 20
percent interest rates and a runaway budget. The Reagan Administration, with considerable help from the Federal Reserve and
its chairman, Paul Volcker, was able to change the country's economic direction and sharply reduce the rate of inflation. President
Reagan has managed to convince a majority of Americans that a
price has to be paid for this change in direction, and many people
have responded favorably and with greater patience than might
have been expected. These are considerable achievements on the
part of the President, although it is hard to deny that the price that
was paid was borne by those least able to afford it.

Business, especially big business, will come out of the recession
far stronger than before. Sharply reduced costs and break-even
points, higher liquidity as a result of lower interest rates and high
stock prices: these will result in significantly higher profits and
competitive positions for most of our large companies. In addition,
the President seems to have luck on his side. The fall in oil and
food prices did much to reduce inflation. Under President Carter,

food and oil prices rose, and there was little he could do about it. Luck should not be sneezed at; we can be impressed both by President Reagan's achievements and by his lucky star. And whatever the shortcomings of his policy, a better one has yet to be spelled out.

However, despite a clear upturn in the economy, not many of our fundamental problems have been addressed; the future is heavily mortgaged and inflows of foreign capital have pushed the dollar to punitively high rates. We are still looking for the formula that will lead to stable growth, low unemployment, reasonably balanced budgets and a reasonably valued currency.

Why are these goals so elusive? The reason, I believe, is that there are fundamental and increasingly acute contradictions in our social and economic structures that we are failing to recognize. The American Century proclaimed by Henry Luce in 1941 lasted only twenty years. From 1965 onward, the United States has been in a period of change which, if anything, is accelerating rather than abating. The difficulties of adjusting to a world we no longer dominate are creating many of the contradictions we are facing today.

We now hear intense arguments about the excessive size of the defense budget, entitlements, taxes and deficits. These are important issues, but they may be the result and not the cause of many of our problems. Instead of relying on economic projections, which turn out to be erroneous as frequently as not, we might more wisely look at some of the underlying trends and try to do something about them.

To begin with, we talk of the obligation to provide, at the very least, the opportunity for employment to all Americans seeking it. We have heard that high technology creates greater requirements for skills and fewer requirements for labor. So does the shift of much of the economy from manufacturing products to providing services. But a conservative political and economic philosophy aggravates this situation by fighting inflation with high unemployment. In England, Germany and the United States, inflation is controlled by high interest rates and slow growth; the by-product of such a policy is an almost permanent high level of unemployment. This may be our most fundamental contradiction.

Next comes education. Two decades after ceasing to dominate

the world industrially, we are trying to bring Japanese methods into our factories. We might do better to bring the quality of Japanese elementary and secondary schools to our own schools. We cannot produce goods efficiently if our children are not taught how to read or count. Insofar as higher education is concerned, neither supply-side nor Keynesian economics will enable us to compete industrially tomorrow when we produce lawyers and MBAs by the tens of thousands instead of teachers, scientists, engineers and chemists. Fortunately for us, Japan is opening its first business school in the near future. This is likely to produce a measurable drop in Japanese productivity. It will, however, not slow them down sufficiently.

The education and judgment of our citizens are not helped by the fact that 150 million TV sets in American homes are now turned on for an average of forty-seven hours per week. This is expected to increase to fifty-four hours during the next few years. At a time when our society needs thoughtful, educated and discriminating voters more than ever before, television programming produces, for the most part, an intellectual desert; and TV news is unable to present complicated, ambiguous or abstract issues.

The goals of state and federal budgets create further contradictions. American cities are falling apart; the needs for public reconstruction are obvious. Basic American industries are besieged by foreign competition on the one hand and recession on the other. We are proposing huge additional defense expenditures, but we are not willing to involve our government more actively in rebuilding our own cities and factories. There is no economic or philosophical difference between the government financing needed for defense and the government financing needed for public investment.

During the last decade there has been a relentless erosion in the vitality of our older cities and of our older industries. Particularly in the northern half of the United States, but also in some parts of the Sunbelt, cities and businesses have suffered together. The result has been high levels of unemployment, erosion of services and the tax base, and emigration to richer parts of the country by those able to move.

Beyond our borders, our policy of high interest rates and slow growth has bankrupted a large part of the world, including Mexico, which now poses a serious problem for U.S. foreign policy.

The response from Mexico is heavy emigration to the United States, both legal and illegal. This new flood of immigrants will compete with other minorities, inner-city blacks and technologically unemployed whites for tomorrow's jobs. The ugly racist demonstrations against immigrants during the recent elections in Germany and France should be cautionary for us. The black community in America will expect whatever political power it can muster to be translated into tangible social and economic gains. It is questionable whether social and economic realities can accommodate such demands, unless we can sustain much stronger and more evenly distributed economic growth.

And while this is happening, the chaotic international monetary system badly needs American leadership, which we refuse to provide while we complain, quite properly, that the unwarranted weakness of the yen and the deutsche mark is destroying American industry by pricing American exports out of the international market, and by displacing American products with imports. The recent economic summit in Williamsburg, Virginia, only pretended to deal with these problems.

Such contradictions can only be dealt with through changes and adjustments in the long-term social trends that work against healthy economic growth—the shift of population and industry away from the northern part of the country, for example, and the decline in the use of industrial capacity and in the quality of American education. Only institutions that can take the long view and act accordingly will be able to bring about the kinds of changes that are required.

If such institutions are to be created, an active government and realistic leaders of both business and labor will have to work jointly to create the political climate in which contradictions can be confronted frankly. This type of cooperation does not imply a sinister corporate-statist conspiracy at the expense of the public or of democratic accountability. Preserving the environment, occupational safety, consumer protection, affirmative action—these and many other issues central to the public interest can and should be an essential part of any arrangements by which business, labor and government cooperate to save the economy. Such cooperative arrangements, in my view, are needed to deal with the budget and with our industrial and regional weaknesses; they are also needed

to coordinate stronger economic growth policies with our allies
and to deal with the Third World debt.

First, the budget. In 1975 New York City did not face up to its
runaway budget problems until the financial market refused to
absorb any more of its notes. Sooner or later the United States will
have a similar problem financing deficits of $200 billion and more.
An occasional deficit, even one as large as the present one, can be
financed and can even be beneficial to recovery, as we are seeing
right now. This, I am sure, is a somewhat recent discovery for
many of my conservative friends. However, another five years of
such deficits, or anything close to them, will push the national debt
up from its present $1.2 trillion to almost double that amount, or
between $2.2 trillion and $2.4 trillion.

The interest alone on such a national debt would be over $200
billion annually. No conceivable growth in gross national product
will enable the United States to afford such interest payments.
Sooner or later, sharp cutbacks will have to be made in the growth
of social costs and military spending; and measures to raise new
revenues will have to be enacted. They should include taxes on
consumption as well as taxes on income. I have, for example,
consistently favored a fifty-cent-per-gallon gas tax which could
produce up to $50 billion a year in revenues. I would combine it
with a minimum corporate income tax of 25 to 30 percent and a
simplified income tax, as proposed by Senator Bill Bradley (New
Jersey) and Representative Richard Gephardt (Missouri), which
carries a maximum rate of 28 percent. Such a tax package should
be phased in as the economy recovers and be designed to produce
about $75 billion annually by the third year. Savings in entitle-
ments and the military should be enacted in order to produce an
equivalent amount. As a result the deficit should be brought to
below $50 billion by the fourth year and, as part of such a compre-
hensive plan, the Federal Reserve could bring interest rates down
by at least another two or three percentage points. A 6 percent
prime rate and long-term rates under 10 percent should be the
result.

Arguments are now being made for policies quite different from
this one: for consumption taxes such as a value-added tax (VAT)
to stimulate investment; for the Laffer curve to justify supply-side
economics; for reductions in taxes on capital; for innumerable

complex reforms to close loopholes or provide incentives. The efficacy and fairness of such measures usually lie in the eye of the beholder. Estimates of revenues raised or lost as a result of these suggestions are almost invariably highly speculative.

I approach the subject, therefore, with skepticism and uncertainty. I believe that taxing all consumption is regressive and counterproductive; in the case of a VAT it only duplicates many state and local taxing schemes that largely depend on sales taxes. Furthermore, the economic health of the United States is too heavily tied to strong consumer spending to risk imposing much heavier taxes on consumption. We can now see, for example, that the failure to stimulate investment after the 1981 tax cuts can only be reversed if very strong levels of consumer spending pull the economy out of the recession.

I believe, however, that heavier taxes on energy can be absorbed by the economy. The effects of a heavy gas tax can be mitigated by rebates to lower-income groups and by consumers' shifting to smaller cars that use gas more efficiently. Sales of big cars are booming again, and companies such as General Motors and Ford are unable to produce cars that meet the current standard for mileage per gallon of gas. Our automobile industry has invested close to $100 billion to build efficient cars over the last decade, yet we are now acting as if the 1973 and 1979 oil shocks never occurred. A stiff gas tax will raise revenues and drive us back to less consumption. Both are desirable.

So in my view is a minimum corporate income tax. We hear that such a tax inhibits investment and growth. But adequate capital formation can be encouraged by lower capital gains taxes, reasonable maximum tax rates for earned and unearned income and, possibly, shorter holding periods on securities transactions. (Most of these measures have been enacted in the last few years.) The corporate income tax is clearly justified on grounds of equity. According to estimates by Data Resources, Inc., corporate earnings for fiscal 1985 will be about $282 billion. The Congressional Budget Office estimates that corporate tax payments in that year will be some $65 billion, or about 23 percent. Such estimates are always tentative; but it seems plausible that a 30 percent tax rate could provide about $20 billion in additional revenue.

At the same time, the entire tax system would benefit from the proposal of Senator Bradley and Representative Gephardt for simplifying both personal and corporate income taxes by reducing the number and amounts of income tax deductions. Their plans for three "steps" of tax levels, with a maximum personal income tax of 28 percent, would be fairer and simpler than our present tax structure, with its innumerable loopholes. One strong advantage of the Bradley-Gephardt plan is that the indexing provision, passed in 1981, could be repealed. The argument that inflation pushes taxpayers into higher and higher brackets loses much of its force if the maximum tax rate is 28 percent. Eliminating indexing would return approximately $6 billion to the Treasury in fiscal year 1985.

In any case, resolving the budget problem cannot be postponed until after the 1984 elections, as some political analysts have suggested. Instead of remaining aloof from the congressional budget process, the President should take the lead on this issue now. Senator Robert Dole has called for a "budget summit," and such a meeting seems to me imperative. It should include the President, the leaders of Congress and the chairman of the Federal Reserve.

If deficits are cut by the kinds of reforms I have suggested, then lower interest rates and a cheaper dollar would permit us to conduct a more coordinated policy for promoting growth in concert with our partners in the Organization for Economic Cooperation and Development (OECD). This would improve our exports and would also facilitate dealing with the $600 billion of Third World debt that is both an economic drag on the West and a continuing danger to our banking system. Stretching out part of this debt at lower interest rates would provide additional stimulus to long-term recovery as well as protect the banking system.

I do not see how this can be done, however, without a major restructuring of the debts of the Third World countries. This would require that Western governments give some guarantees to the banks and that the banks then extend the period of the loans and lower the interest rates paid for them. We now deal with Third World debt by relying on the practice of limited "rollovers" of loans, at extremely high interest rates, in the hope that Western recovery will sufficiently stimulate Third World exports. We hope the poorer countries will then be able to make larger payments on the interest and principal they owe. But we may not attain sufficiently strong Western recovery unless the Third World can import large amounts of Western goods. If we examine Western economic growth during the 1970s, we will find that it was significantly fueled by Western exports to the Third World. Higher exports are equally necessary now, but they are in flat contradiction to the austerity and deflation often imposed on the poorer countries by the International Monetary Fund (IMF). The social pressures created locally as the result of such policies may not be politically tolerable for very long.

Our present policy of renewing loans was highly successful in avoiding disaster last summer when Mexico and Brazil were on the brink of collapse. In the long run, however, it is likely to cause heavier and heavier burdens of debt without providing the financing for sustained growth. From an accountant's point of view, the policy of "rollover" may give the banking system the appearance of having sound balance sheets; it will do nothing to improve the underlying reality. Brazil's acute difficulties in servicing its debt this summer show once again how precarious that reality can be.

Whatever happens, significantly greater credits for the Third World will be required from the Western banking system than the system can now provide. The amounts of money on loan are simply too great. There are two ways of coping with this: either limit the risks posed by existing loans through the type of restructuring I have proposed, or limit the banks' risk on new credits by some form of multinational guarantee. One or the other approach will be needed for adequate future financing to permit Third World and Western growth without unacceptable risks to the banking system. They are two sides of the same coin. Not only must the IMF and the Bank for International Settlements (BIS) continue to work out Third World debt problems, but the activities of the World Bank and the regional organizations should be expanded.

In addition, carefully prepared international monetary conferences should recommend a new system to limit the fluctuation of the main Western trading currencies to manageable levels. Ways should be found for the officials of industrialized countries to collaborate in setting workable targets for the relative values of their currencies. This will be technically difficult to do. The central banks would have to collaborate to some extent on monetary policies and on managing foreign exchange. However, when such different leaders as Helmut Schmidt and Valéry Giscard d'Estaing recommend that a new system for coordinating exchange rates is needed, our own experts should seriously consider what they say.

The United States is currently providing political insurance for virtually all the flight capital in the world at no cost to the insured and at enormous cost to ourselves as a result of an overvalued dollar. It is by no means certain that the lowering of interest rates alone, especially if they are not lowered sharply, will bring the dollar into more rational alignment with the deutsche mark and the yen. Without such a realignment, we will sooner or later inevitably resort to protectionism.* The only long-term alternative to protectionism is an orderly international monetary system, and that will not occur on its own.

When we come to the domestic economy, how can we make sure that inflation will be kept down and employment will be pushed up while the economy grows? I have always been tempted by some kind of legislated, tax-based incomes policy to control inflation— with tax advantages going to those whose wages and prices do not exceed inflation, and tax penalties being applied to those whose wages and prices do. I am inclined to think, however, that this would be cumbersome and impractical to administer fairly.

A different policy that might eventually achieve roughly the same result would encourage the gradual abandonment of multi-year labor contracts, with their built-in and often inflationary cost-of-living allowances. Instead the government could empha-size the advantages of one-year labor contracts that provide for sharing future profits with employees or for bonuses based on productive performance. This would come closer to the Japanese

---

*A possible temporary measure, pending realignment of our currency, would be for the government to impose a variable tariff or tax which would be keyed to a "normal-ized" exchange rate. For instance, if we take 200 yen per dollar as a "normal" rate, the tariff or tax would be zero if the rate is 200 and would move up to 20 percent if the rate is 240. This would obviously not be limited to the yen but would apply to all major currencies that are significantly out of line with the dollar. Such an arrangement is clearly not perfect; it would be far better to have international agreements with respect to main currency values. But it would be better than legislation specifying that products must have "local content" or other permanent trade barriers. It would also eliminate the need for such current arrangements as the so-called "voluntary" restraint agreement on automobiles. In the 1960s we enacted an "interest equalization" tax to improve our balance of payments; what I am suggesting is an "exchange equalization" tax.

or German systems whereby the "spring offensive" negotiations over wage increases in different industries consist of bargaining over the shares of capital and labor in past and future gains. No American government should interfere with the rights of unions and management to make contracts; but government policy could support one-year contracts by making credit available through a new Reconstruction Finance Corporation (RFC) as well as through special trade or tax advantages that would be recommended by a national Economic Development Board. Emphasis on such one-year labor contracts, linked to profit-sharing and higher productivity, could also become part of a new approach to cooperation among business, labor and government that would be the basis for an explicit industrial policy.

There has been a widening—if still vague—agreement that some kind of national industrial policy is needed to arrest the decline of our basic industries and the decay of our cities, and to deal with our failure to compete with other countries. But industrial policy does not mean that a central government agency should "pick winners" by giving promising companies special financing. Nor does it mean that the same agency should simply "bail out losers." It does not mean favoring "high tech" or "low tech." Such a policy should start by recognizing why many of our basic industries are failing and then examining what can be done about it. Our automotive industry needs to be reorganized to make its products comparable in cost and quality with those of its foreign competition. Unrealistic foreign-exchange rates must not be allowed to destroy our domestic manufacturers. Our steel industry has to be modernized so that it can compete with the automated mills abroad. We must maintain a competitive machine-tool industry.

An industrial policy, in my view, should also include a long-term program for energy independence (regardless of short-term reductions in oil prices) and additional government support for technological research and development efforts that individual corporations cannot undertake. Such a policy would call for major investment in transportation systems and harbors to help our exports. And it would mean improving the urban "infrastructure," including schools, mass transit, sewers, etc., as well as the environment, in order to maintain regional balance and to improve the quality of life.

Would such a policy be possible in the United States? It could only be carried out by a President who sought to create a consensus that cut across party lines and had support from major forces in American labor, business and finance. A group of business and labor leaders (of which Irving Shapiro, Lane Kirkland and I are chairmen) has been studying different approaches to a national industrial program. Its work is by no means complete, and many different points of view are being examined. One of the proposals being considered would create a tripartite economic development board, along the lines of the one proposed by President Carter in 1980, which was to have had Lane Kirkland and Irving Shapiro as chairmen. Made up of representatives of business, labor and government, such a board could recommend to the President that assistance be provided to specific industries by extending credits, adjusting taxes and helping with international trade problems.

The board could have as part of its machinery a credit agency modeled after the RFC of the 1930s. Any assistance it gave would have to be based on the principle of shared sacrifice. Labor would make its contribution through wages, benefits and productivity; management through new investment, job security and more efficient working conditions; creditors and investors through matching commitments to any RFC commitments. Trade, tax and credit assistance would always be conditional to appropriate contributions by all parties; and it would be temporary. An expert staff would consider the conditions under which specific industries could become more productive and competitive—if possible—and would provide guidance to the board. Not everyone would qualify for help; bailouts for the inefficient are not part of the plan.*

I am opposed to government planning and to government-owned industries. I believe that the free market is usually the best market. However, the free market is not always adequate and not always right. The free market condemned New York City, Lockheed and Chrysler to bankruptcies that would have been extremely expensive, both in financial and human costs. Limited use of gov-

---

*Some would also argue that, for political and practical reasons, a National Economic Board and a new RFC should be limited to industrial investment and should not, as I would suggest, also invest in regional development, including such public facilities as mass transit and harbors. They could be right, but such issues should be debated.

ernment credit assistance, extensive debt restructuring and the cooperation of business and labor turned them into workable enterprises; but it would have been far better if a competent financing agency had been able to help them face realities earlier.

The cost of such programs need not be burdensome. An RFC could be set up with $5 billion of government capital. It could have the authority to borrow up to ten times its capital, or up to $50 billion, in the public markets. Its borrowings need not be guaranteed by the U.S. government, whose investment would be limited to the initial $5 billion share capital. It could generate between $100 billion and $150 billion total investment, at least, by arranging for its own investment to be augmented with funds from the private sector. In a $3 trillion economy, this hardly amounts to socialism. The RFC, however, is only one of the instruments of national industrial policy; as I have suggested, adjustment of taxes and trade regulations would also be needed. The tripartite board would formulate such measures; and it could only do so in close collaboration with unions, management and other groups. The President and the Congress would have to authorize all of its activities. Far from being undemocratic, the work of such a board would add to the democratic process an element of consultation with the major forces of our society.

An industrial and regional policy could work only if it were accompanied by sound fiscal and monetary national arrangements; but it could, in ways not available to existing agencies, carry out a commitment by the government to help absorb the shocks of rapid adjustment and to maintain a fair social equilibrium. Too many countries successfully competing with us already have something like it. In the long run, a national industrial policy should help us to adapt our training programs and even our education system to what we need. It must try to increase employment for inner-city minorities. It should help to reevaluate the costs and possible tradeoffs of fuller employment. We are going to have to consider plans for an earlier retirement age, for inner-city schools that will be more closely connected with job opportunities, and possibly for some form of national service. Some of these ideas may not work; some may be too expensive. But we will have to consider many changes of the status quo.

If I write with a sense of urgency it is because I fear that rising hopes and expectations at home are continuously encouraged by political promises that cannot be fulfilled. We do not have to bankrupt ourselves to maintain a rational balance of power with the Soviet Union and to protect our vital interests in Central America, the Middle East, Europe or anywhere else. We are not going to war with the Soviet Union; if we are to talk of wars, we should think of the ones that have to be fought at home—against inferior education, racial discrimination, crumbling cities and dying industries, enormous disparities of wealth and privilege. These are struggles we *can* lose. If we do, the result could be a dangerous willingness to experiment with political extremism of the right or the left.

Today's conservatism is an understandable reaction to the recent past, and some of its consequences are healthy ones. Coherent alternatives to it have not been put forward, nor have the gloomiest predictions of bankruptcies and social strife come about. Merely criticizing the unfairness of current policies is not enough. Without realistic alternatives, "fairness" will simply become a code word for social programs and inflation we cannot afford.

If there is an alternative to today's conservatism, it will be a policy committed to maintaining our social gains by promoting economic growth and full employment while delivering balanced budgets; a free enterprise system that does not rely solely on the market to maintain its industrial and regional balance; and a government ready to lead the other Western nations in constructing an orderly financial system and a realistic and consistent foreign policy.

I am not so naïve as to think that such a new approach is likely to emerge soon. It may not be feasible, but it should be tried. It would require four to eight years of a bipartisan Administration in which a Republican or a Democratic President would include opposition leaders in his cabinet and would appoint a genuinely representative group to the kind of economic board I have suggested. When budgets have to be cut or longstanding expectations have to be revised, the blame will have to be widely shared. On a limited scale, that is what the Municipal Assistance Corporation in New York was all about; whatever their shortcomings, the Greenspan and Scowcroft commissions can be seen as steps in the same direction—the former to deal with Social Security, the latter with defense and the MX missile.

Most of the traditional alternatives to the current trend toward conservatism have been discredited by the failures of the Carter Administration, the serious economic problems of the French socialist experiment and the intellectual disgrace of the British Labour Party. The recovery may last, and if it does, the current philosophy of government is likely to prevail for some time. Indeed, if I am wrong and if we have long-term steady growth, the public will support such a philosophy for many years to come, and with good reason. But if I am right, we will face, sooner or later, a national debt of \$2 trillion, a Third World debt of \$1 trillion and an out-of-control budget, and our present domestic, social and economic difficulties will become acute. At that point something will have to change. The time may then come for a new approach emphasizing bipartisanship, cooperation and common sense.

New York Review of Books, August 18, 1983

Excerpts from
Congressional Testimony

IT IS A PRIVILEGE TO TESTIFY BEFORE THIS COMMITTEE on the related questions of industrial policy and the need for a new credit agency to assist in the execution of such policy.

Let me first briefly speak to the question of industrial policy. There is, currently, a great deal of discussion on this subject; I assume that this is only the beginning. Proponents of one form or another of industrial policy feel that our industrial base is being relentlessly eroded. The opposition to it is vigorously expressed by conservatives opposed to government planning and liberals opposed to corporatism and elitism. Industrial policy means different things to different people, somewhat akin to looking at modern art. I should like, briefly, to outline what it means to me as well as what it does not.

First, what should be our national objective? Our objective must be to have a strong, growing, competitive industrial base. This is the antithesis of protectionism, mercantilism and propping up the wasteful and the inefficient. Such an objective is necessary from an economic, social and national security point of view. Lester Thurow, in a recent analysis, showed U.S. productivity growing at 3.3 percent per annum from 1947 to 1965, at 2.4 percent per annum from 1965 to 1972 and at 1.6 percent per annum from 1977 to 1982. This pattern has taken place through several business cycles, inflation and recession, an overvalued dollar and an undervalued dollar. Simply because we are in a recovery, with its improved statistics, does not mean the trend has changed. From 1976 to 1981, productivity in Japan grew at 7.1 percent per annum, in Germany at 3.9 percent per annum and in France at 3.4 percent per annum.

Second, there is no reason to think that the problems encountered by our automotive, machine-tool and metallurgical industries will not be followed by similar problems in our so-called high-technology industries such as computers, telecommunications, aircraft, etc., as well as, ultimately, the nonmanufacturing and service sector. It is not only because of the dollar/yen relationship that the Japanese have captured 70 percent of the 64K RAM semiconductor market and 100 percent of the video cassette recorder market. There are more fundamental forces at work.

I would, therefore, argue as follows:

- A more coherent set of industrial policies (and *not* one overarching industrial policy) should be a part of our national and international economic posture.
- These have to fit into a sound national fiscal and monetary policy mix. This means that budget deficits have to be reduced significantly and that monetary policy has to be relaxed and interest rates lowered.
- These industrial policies have to be based on the need for more cooperation, more competitiveness and more coordination.
- Our main competitors on the world markets, Japan and Germany, have significantly more institutionalized industrial policies than we do. I believe that we should have the full panoply of policies available to our competitors. This is not the case today.

The argument about whether or not to pursue industrial policies has an *Alice in Wonderland* aura when one considers the fact that we have a number of such policies. Already there are steel trigger pricing and quotas, "voluntary" automobile restrictions with Japan, tariffs on motorcycles, loan guarantees to synthetic fuel plants, etc. Many of these policies, however, are uncoordinated and provide results that have little to do with the objective: e.g., steel companies using their benefits to acquire oil companies instead of modernizing their facilities. This indicates that policies to be effective have to be coordinated, and that they have to be targeted sufficiently to bring about the desired objective. That objective is not to protect inefficient industries at the expense of the American consumer, but to assist American industry to be more aggressively competitive, both in terms of price and quality, with its foreign competitors. This will benefit customers, employees and shareholders.

This country has had considerable success with targeted industrial policies in which the government and the private sector worked together. We became the world's dominant agricultural producers as a result of deliberate policies which included credit assistance through the Rural Electrification Administration, and a whole series of interrelated policies. The Reconstruction Finance Corporation, before and during World War II, helped create a number of industries including much of the aluminum industry and the synthetic rubber industry. The RFC went out of business after World War II when the postwar boom eliminated the need for its financial assistance. Many of the RFC's offspring, however, continue to function to this date. The Commodity Credit Corporation, the REA, the Small Business Administration, the Federal National Mortgage Association all perform valuable services in our economy and bear witness to the benefits of intelligent action. Many other examples—the financing of western railroads with federal land grants, the creation of the Tennessee Valley Authority—are proof that government involvement can be vitally helpful.

Few people would argue today that we do not have considerable industrial problems. The real argument comes down to an evaluation of risk: Is there a greater risk in trying to do something or is there a greater risk in doing nothing? To me, the significantly greater risk is doing nothing.

In recommending that something be done, however, I am also mindful of the failures that have occurred here and abroad, and I will attempt to reduce those risks in my recommendations. Policies of government-owned enterprises and government planning have a history of occasional successes together with numerous failures in Great Britain, France and Italy. There is no need to repeat those experiments here. However, we have seen here in the last decade examples of what can be accomplished with the correct combination of policies and actions. Lockheed, New York City and Chrysler were all doomed to bankruptcy by the financial markets. They are all thriving today as a result of limited government credit assistance and drastic restructuring; these are some of the principles I advocate.

First, we need to establish a set of principles. These would include:

- The principle of cooperation between business, labor and government. Clearly, adversarial positions among these and other groups in our society will exist part of the time; but in areas where industrial policies will be applied, the principle of cooperation will have to override.
- The principle of government assistance and not of government coercion. Any plans recommended to the President and the Congress can only be carried out with the relevant industry participating in their execution. Government's role would be to provide part of the assistance on condition that contributions by other parties (labor, banks, suppliers, stockholders, management, etc.) are forthcoming. Government would not unilaterally formulate the plans or impose them.
- The policy tools to be made available must include the full panoply of tax, trade, credit and regulation. All would be recommended to the President and the Congress, subject to appropriate approval or legislation and subject to periodic congressional review.

Whether you believe that our industrial problems are overwhelming or only very important, there has been a widening—if still vague—agreement that some national focus is needed to improve the performance of our important industries and the physical condition of many of our cities, to provide greater future employment opportunities and to compete more effectively with other countries. . . .

One of the questions asked in this connection is: Why do we need a Development Bank; are the capital markets not available to viable projects? Why not just have a tripartite board? The answer is that the capital markets do not negotiate concessions among various parties. The Chrysler unions, suppliers and banks all made significant concessions, vital to Chrysler's return to health, as a result of conditions imposed as part of the government's $1.5 billion credit guaranteed. The same was true of New York City. The amount of credit assistance (whether by direct investment, loans, guarantees, etc.) can and should be limited. At least 50 percent of any investment should come from the private markets, as an ongoing check. But the leverage created can be enormous; for instance, the Municipal Assistance Corporation and

New York City were able to arrange a total of almost $12 billion of unguaranteed credit using the $1.5 billion federally guaranteed credit line as a linchpin. As an ultimate check, I would recommend an automatic sunset provision for such a credit agency after, say, ten years. . . .

Industrial policies are not a panacea. The problems of black unemployment, inner-city blight, regional shifts and educational standards will all have to be faced up to as part of a national program of recovery. But industrial policies can help in one area and, if successful, the spillover into some of these other areas could be significant. Once parties with conflicting interests learn to cooperate in one area, surprising things can happen in the others.

In summary, I believe we should act before it is too late, which may already be true in some cases. I believe we have little to lose and much to gain by trying to promote the principles of cooperation, sharing of sacrifice and dedication to greater excellence and competitiveness. I am not afraid of the proposition that government involvement can be a positive factor; I would go further and say that, in this case, there is an affirmative obligation for government involvement. To those who say that there is no need for such efforts because everything will be just fine when our macroeconomic policies are rational, and when the dollar and interest rates are down, I would reply that their predictions might be wrong. It would not be the first time. Even if all these wonderful things happen, we will have lost little by adopting more coordinated industrial policies. And if, as I believe, we will still face many of these problems under better macroeconomic policies and with a cheaper dollar, we will have policies in place to try to deal with them.

There is no doubt in my mind that without sound tax, budget and monetary policies we are doomed to failure. But, I am also convinced that even under the best of circumstances, we are going to face problems in industry and employment that will require stronger action than mere faith in the status quo.

Excerpts from testimony before the House Subcommittee on Economic Stabilization, Committee on Banking, Finance and Urban Affairs, U.S. House of Representatives, Washington, D.C., September 14, 1983

Chapter Two

THE READER WILL FIND FOUR RELATED PIECES IN THIS chapter. They cover the overall state of our banking system, a proposal to stretch out the Third World debt and an amplification thereto, and finally an argument for the bankruptcy of Poland. These pieces were written during the year April 1982 to April 1983, and at the time of this writing, I have not changed my overall views; if anything, I hold to them more decisively.

In the fall of 1982 I wrote a piece for the *New York Review of Books* on the international debt problem and the state of the banking system. This was a subject that had troubled me for some time, but about which I was loath to write. It is a delicate subject, involving public institutions, where one is likely to be damned whether right or wrong. I decided, however, that the problem would not go away and that no one involved in economic affairs could avoid its exploration.

"The State of the Banks" was published in November 1982, sandwiched between an argument I made for the bankruptcy of Poland in the *Wall Street Journal* in April of that year (the last item in this chapter) and an essay for *Business Week,* based on congressional testimony, in February 1983 (this chapter's second item).

The present economic recovery in the United States has reduced some of the pressure existing at the time I wrote these pieces. The boom in the stock market and the lowering of interest rates have allowed many corporations to improve their liquidity and financial institutions to improve their portfolios. Nevertheless, many uncertainties still exist.

These essays have generated a certain amount of controversy, especially among my friends in the banking community. That is quite understandable, since I am suggesting fairly radical departures from the status quo. I wish to see the banks sound and solid, and in the best possible position to finance the growth in the world economy, for it is an absolute necessity that they be able to do so. This is not inconsistent with my conviction that the Soviet Union should participate in the financing of Eastern Europe, even if it means the bankruptcy of Poland, and with my conviction that such overall growth requires significant stretchouts of world debt. I believe this can be managed with due regard to the health of the banking system. I strongly believe that regulatory limits should be set on the exposure that is acceptable in any one country, just as regulatory limits exist with respect to any one borrower. I believe the risk of default or repudiation by a sovereign government, which can be brought about by unpredictable political and social events, is a real risk. Even though the probability of its happening may be small, its impact could be so severe that it seems reckless not to try to ensure against it.

The question of whether it is appropriate for private U.S. banks to lend to foreign governments has yet to be debated. In the case of communist governments, I feel strongly that it is not appropriate and should be handled on a government-to-government basis.

The need for an orderly foreign-exchange system seems to me greater every day. This is an exceedingly complicated subject. I believe there is a requirement for relatively stable relationships between the main trading currencies (dollar, sterling, deutsche mark, French franc, yen) in order to permit rational business planning for investment, borrowing and trade. Maintaining such relationships, however, requires more than simple agreements among central banks to intervene in the foreign-exchange markets in order to maintain these currencies within limits. This is now done within the European Monetary System. It would require, in addition, coordination in

managing monetary policy so that international capital flows
will be accommodated by corresponding money supply actions
to avoid wild swings in interest rates. This is an exceedingly
complicated and technical subject, and an international
commission of experts, headed by men such as Arthur Burns
and Helmut Schmidt, should be convened and asked for
recommendations.

I believe the problem of Third World debt to be one of the
critical issues of this decade. It will affect the ability of the
West to achieve its own economic recovery and, equally
important, can have political implications all over the world. It
is, like the related issue of exchange-rate stability, an
exceedingly complicated technical issue. It is also, quite
understandably, controversial.

As of this writing, Mexico appears to be making significant
progress toward recovery; Brazil is under considerable
economic and social pressure; Venezuela is trying to postpone
the issue until its elections; Chile is undergoing political
convulsions; Argentina incarcerated the head of its central
bank for failure to defend the national interest; the rest of the
world is in various stages of recovery or disarray. Nonetheless,
these are all holding operations and a great deal of luck
together with a world-wide economic recovery far stronger
than I anticipate would be required for it all to work out
without major surgery. We may wind up with the worst of all
worlds: no repayment of the debts combined with a politically
radicalized, anti-American region extending from Mexico to
Argentina.

A clarification of my position on Third World debt consists
in a letter I wrote in April 1983 to Andrew Knight, editor of
The Economist. The Economist had been running a series of
articles and editorials on this issue, and had commented on my
proposal and a related one by Professor Peter B. Kenen of
Princeton, which would involve the purchase, at a discount, of
some of the Third World loans held by the banks. I felt the
need for clarification and wrote the letter included herein.

I have not changed my mind on the subject of the bankruptcy of Poland, which I discussed in a 1982 essay. Unfortunately, the scenario that I outlined has gradually unfolded. General Wojciech Jaruzelski released Lech Walesa from jail, replaced martial law with similarly restrictive civil laws, crushed Solidarity and expects new credits. The Western banks will become more deeply involved and the Soviet Union will not contribute any support whatsoever. The discussions involving the restructuring of the Polish debt taking place at the time of this writing confirm my worst fears. The old credits will be extended for ten years, with a lengthened grace period, and the interest to be paid by Poland will be lent back to the extent of 65 percent. This means providing ten-year loans at about 5 percent interest to a bankrupt communist government. This cannot in any sense be in our national interest.

From an overall point of view, we are, as of this writing, trying to limit the strength of our economic recovery in fear of a recurrence of inflation. I believe that the risk of deflationary damage in the rest of the world is the greater risk and that we should opt for stronger growth and easing of credit at this time, even at the risk of somewhat higher inflation.

The State of
the Banks

THE VITALITY OF WESTERN ECONOMIES IS BASED, IN IM-
portant ways, on the health of our credit system. This system
depends on the actual financial strength of large Western banks
and on the financial and fiscal policies of Western governments, as
well as on public psychology. Today, for a variety of reasons, we
are witnessing a loss of confidence in our banking system which,
if allowed to continue, could have serious repercussions.

The word "credit" derives from the Latin *credere,* to believe.
Prudence on the part of lenders and borrowers has to be supported
by the general belief on the part of consumers and depositors that
the system will work. Today this belief has become perilously
fragile. It is not fragile, as some bankers may believe, because
"there is too much loose talk about the problem." By now, every
responsible businessman should know that the word "crisis" is
newsworthy and that press and TV reporting make it utterly impossible to avoid serious questions about the banking system, even
if it were desirable to do so. Furthermore, it is undeniable that both
the known facts and the potential problems argue against a policy
of hoping to muddle through with a little bit of luck. The risk of
inaction is simply too great.

During the last decade, major changes have occurred in the
organization and functioning of Western economies, world trade
and the distribution of wealth among nations. All of these changes,
in one form or another, are causes for the enormous pressures that
weigh on our banking system.

The first of these causes lies in the international economy. The
world today appears to have entered a deflationary cycle. For the
first time since World War II every industrially developed country
is in various stages of recession. Unemployment levels are rising

and inflation rates are coming down. But real interest rates are still prohibitively high and financial pressures are causing cutbacks in industry and government. In the United States the fight against inflation appears to be successful; we may, however, find that success carries a heavy price. The impact of U.S. deflation on the rest of the world is staggering: recession, unemployment and collapsing raw material prices are a world-wide phenomenon. There can be no world-wide recovery without a U.S. recovery; the United States has to be the locomotive.

Second, the demise in 1971 of the arrangements made at Bretton Woods in 1944 caused the breakdown of an international monetary system that made the years between 1945 and 1971 among the most successful in the history of monetary management. Indeed, for all countries, rich and poor, this was the most fruitful period in the history of the world. Harold Lever, who has one of the most brilliant financial minds in England, said in a December 1981 speech: "Bretton Woods was itself the greatest single achievement in terms of creating an institution which would bridge the growing interdependence of the world and national decisions." The effect of the Bretton Woods agreements was to make the dollar the world's reserve currency, against which every other major currency was pegged. When the Bretton Woods system broke down with the floating of the dollar in 1971, no country or group of countries was able to assume the responsibilities that had been carried by the United States; no international currency was substituted for the dollar. Bretton Woods was replaced by nothing, and the OPEC oil shock of 1973 was superimposed on a world monetary system that had been completely disrupted.

Third was the distress caused by the rise of oil prices after 1973. OPEC created huge, long-term balance-of-payments deficits in many countries whose economies were shaken by high energy costs they could not pay. Lacking an adequate monetary system, the rich and poor nations had to resort to the policy of "bank recycling." This was a process whereby OPEC oil producers deposited their surplus cash with Western banks, which then lent the money partly to poorer non-oil-producing countries in need of credit. There was, at the time, no alternative to bank recycling other than direct OPEC lending to Third World countries, and OPEC loans to such countries remained relatively small.

However, the effect of bank recycling was to lend more and more to less and less credit-worthy borrowers; it meant ever greater burdens on weak borrowers. Running as high as $100 billion per year, OPEC surpluses were deposited with Western banks which lent part of them throughout the world. No doubt both some of the banks and some of the borrowing countries were incautious and overeager in arranging these loans. By 1982 the Third World's debt reached $500 billion, most of it in the form of short-term debt.

Fourth, during the seventies, "détente" governed our relations with the Soviet Union and Eastern Europe. Mutual economic interests would, it was thought, help create an atmosphere in the Soviet Union that would restrain its geopolitical behavior while a step-by-step process of limiting and reducing arms could take place. Encouraged by their governments, Western banks lent Eastern Europe over $50 billion between 1972 and 1982. The collapse of both détente and the Eastern European economies abruptly halted this process.

Last but not the least important was our appetite for credit in the United States itself. Growth and inflation were the dominant economic trends of the 1970s, interrupted here and there by recession in one Western country or another, but never at precisely the same time among all Western countries. The high rates of inflation sharply lowered real interest rates and permitted heavy borrowers to "service" their debts—i.e., pay both interest and installments of the principal—with cheaper currency. The conviction grew among many business leaders, especially in the United States, that inflation was here to stay. As a result, the use of credit soared. In 1950 the average U.S. corporation had $43 of operating income to meet each dollar of interest payments; today the average corporation has less than $4 to meet each dollar of such payments. Liquid assets are down to 24 percent of short-term liabilities, half of what they were during the 1950s. The ratios of short-term debt to long-term debt on corporate balance sheets have climbed from 40 percent in the 1950s to 70 percent today.

Short-term debt has been used not only to provide long-term capital assets such as new plants but much else besides, including real estate and other speculations, and larger and larger corporate takeovers. Normal prudence would have required much greater use of long-term credits, but their high interest cost was often deemed prohibitive. As a result, many American corporations under heavy obligation to repay short-term loans now find themselves short of "liquidity"—cash or assets convertible into cash; and the banks, the providers of short-term credit, have become more and more "exposed"—i.e., are owed increasingly large sums in relation to their own assets.

It is dangerous to generalize. Not all banks are in trouble; not all countries pose similar credit risks. However, the interdependence of the international monetary system is such that, in some respects, the system is only as strong as its weakest links. We cannot, for instance, ignore the situation of Canadian banks. The absence of any legal lending limits, a government policy of financing Canadian repurchase of energy assets, and the collapse of the local economy—all have contributed to the dangerously overextended condition of the Canadian banking system. German banks have made large and often risky loans in Eastern Europe; Belgium's second largest bank faces a $200 million loss with an obscure Saudi foreign-exchange trading firm. These are matters of concern to all of us even though the respective central banks have the direct responsibility as ultimate lenders.

Completely outside the system is a network of banks for which no central bank is directly responsible. The best current example of such "rogue" banks is the Italian Banco Ambrosiano, in which the Vatican is reported to have lost over $1 billion and whose Luxembourg subsidiary owes Western banks over $400 million. Nobody really knows the size of the outstanding loans of banks in such tax-shelter havens as the Cayman Islands. It could be significant.

When New York City faced its crisis, some argued against full disclosure of the magnitude of the city's problems, above all its inability to borrow more money in view of widespread skepticism about its ability to pay. It was argued, not without some justification, that disclosure would bring on the very crisis the city was trying to prevent. Those of us who were asked to help the city chose to disclose the facts while at the same time coming forth with a plan to resolve the crisis. It was a correct, if probably inevitable, decision. The same must now be done on a much vaster, more complicated scale.

The unknown in many ways is scarier than the known. Rumors about the shaky condition of this or that bank are creating financing difficulties for some American banks, notwithstanding the widely shared judgment that the Federal Reserve would never permit a major American bank to default on its obligation to depositors. It is imperative that steps be taken, rapidly, to restore confidence in the banking system, both domestically and internationally.

The steps outlined here are not necessarily a "solution" to the problem; there may be no solution short of a decade of strong, world-wide economic growth. They are, rather, intended to suggest a coordinated process that would shore up the system and avoid a crisis. Several discrete issues will have to be faced very soon if, during the next three to five years, we are to avoid a financial breakdown.

1) *The U.S. banking system must be strengthened.* According to the Federal Reserve, as of May 1982, U.S. banks have lent over $300 billion abroad. This includes $200 billion in Latin America, the Third World and Eastern Europe. To put these numbers in perspective, it is worth noting that the total equity of the thirty largest U.S. bank holding companies as of mid-1982—i.e., the value of their assets above their total liabilities—was about $40 billion. American banks are major participants in Mexico's $80 billion of external debt, as well as Brazil's $60 billion and Argentina's $40 billion. The risks to American banks of an unexpected default by these and other countries would therefore be grave ones.

Complicating the situation are certain illusions and accounting practices that shape many banking decisions. It is, in my judgment, an illusion to think that no sovereign country will default on its external debt because it would become a pariah in the international financial community. Default or a repudiation of debt could occur as a result of radical political changes (as is possible in literally any Latin American country) or geopolitical decisions (as might be the case in Eastern Europe).

At the same time, the prevailing accounting practices show more than a few banks making higher operating profits by "rolling over," or extending, highly questionable debts from borrowers like Poland, thereby avoiding writing them off as a loss. This practice creates a dangerous illusion. A bank's operating results appear to be improved as it takes on greater and greater debts from risky countries, and the bank becomes more and more the prisoner of the borrower.

For loans within the United States the risks, although significant, are usually more manageable. First of all, the legal lending limit allows an American bank to lend no more than 10 percent of its capital to any one borrower. This restriction, however, does not apply to "country risk," namely the aggregate of loans to any one country. By lending to several different government entities, as well as to private businesses, in a foreign country, a bank may put at risk a much greater proportion of its capital. It is no secret that several major American banks have an important share of their capital on loan in Mexico, Brazil and Argentina. Furthermore, because the risks in the less developed countries and Eastern Europe are more subject to foreign political decisions, they are also less predictable and more sudden than the domestic equivalent.

The fact that International Harvester may go bankrupt has been known for some time. The same is true of Dome Petroleum in Canada and AEG in Germany. In one way or another such companies can usually be reorganized. Certain of their assets can be sold off; the shrunken remainder of the company can be merged with another company, or run independently; and so a rescue plan can come about. The potential bank losses, although severe, do not pose a danger to the system. There have been surprises, of course: the failure of Penn Square Bank in Oklahoma and of Drysdale Securities and Lombard-Wall in New York, not to mention the Hunt silver caper. These were sizable cases of acquisition of very risky short-term debt; but they could be contained. Excessive international debt requires additional safety precautions.

We now have only one half of a safety net for our American banks: the Federal Reserve system, which can supply liquidity to a bank, as a lender of last resort. We need, in addition, an organization that can supply capital as an investor of last resort. I have, for some time, argued for the creation of a modern version of the federal Reconstruction Finance Corporation of the 1930s. An RFC could be such an investor, as it was originally to thousands of banks and other financial institutions.

The possible need for *capital,* as opposed to *liquidity,* could arise out of a major default that required, for legal and accounting reasons, a writeoff of such magnitude as to impair a major bank's capital, and therefore its ability to lend and function. The RFC, or a similar institution, would have the authority to acquire preferred stock of banks with capital problems. The RFC would thus both supply capital and relieve the danger to a bank caused by a sudden, major default. It would permit an orderly settlement of the bank's obligations. It would give our banks protection against a sudden political decision in foreign countries to renege on payments or even to practice financial blackmail in the form of a threat to bring down American banks unless more credit were extended. The mere existence of such an arrangement under the RFC would help remove the present widespread concern about the soundness of our banks, which is clearly detrimental to an economic recovery. Any investment by the RFC would have to be part of an overall plan, under the control of the Federal Reserve, whereby standby loans would be provided by the Fed and more permanent capital by the RFC.

This is a limited, but direct, form of federal intervention in the banking system. An alternative would be less visible but more open-ended. If a major foreign loan were suddenly in default, it could be assumed by the Federal Reserve at its "discount window," that is, the channel through which the Federal Reserve regularly lends money to U.S. banks. Like the RFC, this approach would seem to require legislation, since the Fed can now only make loans to member banks against full collateral. It is, however, a workable approach to the problem and could be part of a program to give the banks time to recognize the impact on their capital.

I recently advocated a plan that would acknowledge the bankruptcy of Poland and provide that Polish loans held by the private banks be taken over by their respective national banks. I proposed that the central banks pay the private banks fifty cents on the dollar in assuming a debt that the Polish government has no realistic prospect of paying. This would be essential to the safety of some German banks. The principle of both the interventions I have mentioned is the same, whatever the numbers. And the principle underlines the political question that must be faced, sooner or later, of who will pay the ultimate costs if a bank faces failure. Both the taxpayers and the bank's stockholders will have to assume a part of such costs if the banking system is to be protected; what must be worked out will be the proportion of costs each will share.

These are steps that would shore up the domestic banking system insofar as the past is concerned. As to the future, clearly some changes in regulation are required. The most obvious would be to extend the principle of the legal limit now applicable to one borrower to "foreign-country risk" as well. An American bank may lend an amount equivalent to no more than 10 percent of its capital to IBM; but it can lend an aggregate 100 percent of its capital or more to various Mexican entities. Clearly this makes no sense. Whether the limit to a foreign country should be 10 percent, or perhaps 20 percent, as is the case with Japanese banks, is arguable. The principle seems to me unquestionable, and should be implemented as soon as possible.

2) *The international institutions must be strengthened.* Clearly, the United States must support the International Monetary Fund (IMF), the World Bank and the Bank for International Settlements. Each of these institutions draws on funds provided by the richer nations to supply credit to countries in economic difficulty. Doubling the IMF's capacity to lend money from its present $60 billion or so does not seem excessive. Whether it is done directly or partly by a special emergency fund, as the Reagan Administration suggests, is a matter of choice. The real question concerns the role of the IMF in the present world economy.

When New York City faced bankruptcy, we were able to reestablish its credit by imposing austerity measures and refinancing its short-term debt through state institutions such as the Municipal Assistance Corporation and the Emergency Financial Control Board. A buoyant economy, coupled with these austerity measures, allowed us to succeed without unacceptable social trauma.

The IMF can be seen as a world-wide version of MAC, but it will try to impose the same sort of austerity program in a world-wide economic environment not of growth but of contraction and deflation. In many countries seeking IMF loans, the gulf between social classes is enormous and the prevailing political realities may deny the possibility of the austerity measures the IMF requires. Increasing radicalism, demagogy and anti-Western agitation may be the result. We must remember the evolution of Germany in reaction to the Dawes and Young plans of the 1920s, which were meant to finance German World War I reparations. That Germany's national wealth was seen as being drained off to pay back foreign banks helped to create the climate in which Hitler took power in 1933.

It is this inherent contradiction between the measures needed to refinance the past and those needed to provide for the future that creates the greatest present challenge. The IMF, in exchange for financial assistance designed to restructure debt, demands that the countries it helps institute stringent anti-inflationary measures. It asks for currency devaluations to stimulate exports, reductions of local subsidies for foodstuffs and other products, less support for nationalized industries, and lower domestic budgets. These are difficult measures to implement in the best of times. In times of hardship they are explosive. Several years ago Anwar Sadat tried to impose such a program in Egypt; the resulting social turmoil forced him to abandon the project. Recent speeches at the United Nations by the presidents of Brazil and Mexico referred rather ominously to the consequences of imposing austerity on Third World countries. The possibility that some among them may decide to default rather than accept the IMF's demands should not simply be dismissed.

Along with recession, a dramatic contraction of world credit is taking place. *Business Week* recently estimated that a year from now no more than 100 big banks (down from 1,100 today) will be actively participating in large syndicated loans to foreign countries. Jacques de Larosière, managing director of the IMF, recently pleaded with the banks not to withdraw from the international credit markets. The facts of life, however, dictate otherwise. As of the end of 1981, *Fortune* magazine reported the aggregate capital of the 100 largest banking companies outside the United States to be $116 billion. This capital, together with the capital of U.S. banks, is unlikely to be adequate to supply the domestic needs as well as the international credit requirements of today's world. Unless concerted effort is made soon, the contraction in credit taking place right now will result in a further decline in international trade and in raw material prices and is likely to cause further deterioration in the already fragile international credit structure.

It will be most difficult to bridge this contradiction between the growing need for credit and its sharp decline. Only a process of close cooperation among Western government and central banks, commercial banks and international organizations will have any chance of success. Sizable new credits from the banking system, extensions of existing debts, temporary moratoriums—all these measures will be required. To carry some of them out may require government guarantees as well as the involvement of both national and international institutions. The private banks, alone, cannot carry the burden. If current economic conditions continue for a year or so many countries will not be able to afford the interest on their loans, much less any part of the principal.

Any process intended to rescue both debtors and creditors must be carefully managed if it is to have a chance of success. In New York City we were able to manage the process by gathering around the same table representatives of those institutions needed to provide a solution: the state, the city, the banks, the labor unions. On an international scale such collaboration would be far more difficult, but something analogous will have to be undertaken.

A conference of creditor nations should be called to discuss not only current problems but the new structures needed to manage long-term solutions to them. If the industrially developed world is to increase substantially the assets of the IMF, an executive committee representing these countries should have a greater say in IMF policy. This would not be to the liking of many Third World countries, but credit is a scarce commodity; it will be politically necessary for the West to keep greater control of it. To deal with internal credit effectively, responsibility for different regions should be created. Western European countries should take the lead in working out refinancing plans for the debts of Eastern Europe; Soviet participation in such plans should be a sine qua non, since the U.S.S.R. has been benefiting from loans to Eastern Europe while staying aloof from the problem of repayment. The United States and Japan should take the lead in refinancing arrangements with Latin America. The Europeans and OPEC might have a major part in dealing with Africa and with nations in some other parts of the Third World.

There is, unfortunately, no "solution" to this problem. Of the $500 billion in loans to the poorer nations from the Western banking system, much will never come back; or if it does, it will come back over a very long period indeed. The classic method for the repayment of such excessive credit was a combination of inflation and growth. Both have been replaced by Western economic strategies of fighting inflation through equally classic methods of retrenchment and stagnation. Something will have to give. It is quite possible that fundamental changes in some Western countries will come about. The inevitable government involvement required to keep some of the banks afloat could lead, in Canada for instance, to the nationalization of some banks as the only way to maintain confidence. The past may impose a heavy price for excessive credit, but we have no pleasant alternatives to recognizing this.

3) *The international monetary system must be reexamined.* Since the demise of Bretton Woods, we have replaced an international system based on fixed exchange rates—which posed many problems—with a system based on floating rates, with even greater problems. The wild fluctuations in foreign exchange rates, speculative raids on individual currencies, the uncontrolled growth of the Eurodollar market—all have contributed to world-wide inflation and destabilization. Cooperation among the United States, Japan and the Western European governments to synchronize economic policies geared to sound growth is now vital.

So are commitments by their respective central banks to cooperate in controlling movements of currency. The pound sterling in 1976 dropped by a third; by 1980 it had gone up 50 percent. In 1981 it dropped 20 percent in six months. During 1978 the yen gained 45 percent against the dollar and the deutsche mark 27 percent. They have both gone down dramatically since then. There should be clear and public commitments among the major central banks to maintain their respective currencies within specific limits as long as their respective governments maintain rational economic policies. One way to do this would be to expand the European monetary system to include the United States, Japan and possibly Canada. Such close cooperation is obviously inconsistent with the American sanctions against European governments and companies involved in the construction of the Soviet gas pipeline; it would certainly permit, however, negotiations aimed at tightening European subsidies, through cheap credit, of exports to the Soviet Union or anywhere else.

Such a program must also include a greater effort on the part of those who, until now, have not pulled their weight in providing credit and assuming risks: the Soviet Union in Eastern Europe; the larger OPEC producers in the Third World. It also, quite clearly, requires policies more aggressively geared to growth, which is the only long-term remedy for the current disease. The risk of somewhat higher inflation levels has to be recognized and compensated for.

The importance of Bretton Woods can be seen in the deterioration of the international economic situation since its demise. The world is getting smaller and the stakes are getting larger; a new system must be put in place quickly.

It took fifteen years for New York City to come to the edge of bankruptcy; it took six years to work out the arrangements that avoided it. Many shared responsibility for the crisis: politicians, banks, unions, voters. All who created the problem participated in the solution. So it must be today. Our banking system is one of the most precious assets of our economy and of the free society itself. Recognizing the dangers facing it does not require us to engage in a witch hunt to allocate blame for a situation for which changing world-wide economic, social and political conditions are as much at fault as anything else. The problem will not go away; its dimensions are too great. It has to be faced with cooperation, courage and candor. If the Western governments together with their financial institutions can muster those qualities, then, with some luck and a great effort, a crisis in the banking system can be avoided during the coming decade.

New York Review of Books, November 4, 1982

A Plan for Stretching Out Global Debt

FEBRUARY 1983

LAST YEAR BROUGHT ABOUT A SHARPENING PERCEPTION that the international economic problems the world faces could escalate into crisis at any time, and that the industrial nations have to work together to resolve these problems. The United States now recognizes that, whether we like it or not, we live in an interconnected world. Mexico's default crisis, followed shortly by that of Brazil, produced a relaxation of Federal Reserve monetary policy, American support for substantially increasing the lending resources of the International Monetary Fund, and a multinational rescue effort, led by the United States, the IMF and a group of commercial banks. The fact that between the Ottawa Conference of 1981 and the present time the U.S. government changed its attitude is probably the most important improvement in the world situation.

On both sides of the Atlantic, suggestions are heard for a new Bretton Woods meeting and for coordinated Western growth. Both arise from a recognition that although we have bought time in dealing with the international financial situation, a significant danger still exists.

The disarray among OPEC countries creates an opportunity for the West and the Third World. This opportunity is obscured by legitimate worry about the banking system. There is also worry about whether the large borrowers that are also oil producers, such as Mexico, will be able to service their debts. Despite such concerns, a significant and orderly reduction in oil prices is clearly in the interest of world-wide economic recovery and noninflationary growth. The opportunity to undo some of the appalling damage to the world's economy inflicted by the 1973 and 1979 oil shocks must not be allowed to slip by. We can handle the problems caused by falling oil prices more easily than the stagnation caused by high ones.

Under the management of the IMF and the Bank for International Settlements, the West was able to avoid a financial crisis in 1982. But to continue to forestall crises we need the following:

- for the time being, a substantially beefed-up IMF, together with a continuation of bank loan reschedulings
- long-term, low-interest rescheduling of much of the Third World's debt in order to give these countries economic breathing room
- a stable international monetary system, together with international trade policies that are as open as possible

In looking at the international financial scene, we must recognize a fundamental fact: We have become the prisoners of our debtors. Poland, Mexico, Argentina, Brazil, and now Romania have all unilaterally defaulted on their debts and are, in effect, dictating rescheduling terms to our banks. Poland has now gone so far as to include $3 billion of 1983 debts that will not be repaid as a savings in its current budget. The acquiescence of our banks in rescheduling both interest and principal is now taken for granted. Except for the debt in Eastern Europe, our banks really have no choice.

The reality of the situation is that a significant part of the approximately $700 billion now lent to the Third World and the Eastern bloc will come back, if ever, only over a long period. Instead of maintaining the fiction that these are short-term, high-interest loans and asking the banks to increase their commitments, it might be better, both for lenders and borrowers, to create a mechanism that would stretch existing loans out to twenty-five to thirty years, with an interest rate of, say, 6 percent. This would provide enormous immediate relief to the borrowing countries without changing the economic reality of these credits. The saving on interest costs alone could amount to $15 billion to $20 billion annually and would reduce the current pressure for additional credits from an overstretched banking system. Together with the remaining short- or medium-term debt, the schedule for principal repayments could be tailored country by country to reduce debt service costs to 25 to 30 percent of exports. This could be combined with commodity agreements and more practical IMF oversight of new credits aimed at development and growth.

The problem, while much greater in magnitude and infinitely more complicated, is not unlike that faced by New York City in 1975. Then the solution included forming an independent state agency, the Municipal Assistance Corporation of New York (MAC), that could convert the city's short-term debt into long-term debt. This was possible because the state allocated a tax revenue stream, which the city could not touch and which assured that the debt service would be paid.

Debt-heavy countries need the same conversion of short-term to long-term debt. The fact that they are sovereign nations complicates the solution. Still, some international agency, such as the IMF (which is essentially a worldwide MAC) or a new organization, could help those debtor countries establish a revenue stream tied to sales of their commodities or other kinds of income in a way that would service their long-term bonds in an orderly and credible manner. Such a new agency would undoubtedly have to carry some form of guarantee by Western governments.

I am aware that such a program might involve the recognition of significant cost and balance-sheet losses. A twenty-five-year, 6 percent loan is worth considerably less, on its face, than a short-term, 13 percent loan. The allocation of such costs among bank stockholders, taxpayers and countries would be the subject of difficult negotiations. However, if they were successful, all parties would see daylight at the end of the tunnel.

The mechanism for such a stretch-out will not be difficult to construct once it is decided how to allocate the costs. We should now consider the creation of a subsidiary of the World Bank or of the IMF or a totally new institution, guaranteed by the Western governments, that could acquire the banks' credits in exchange for long-term, low-interest bonds of its own. The new entity would become the substitute creditor to the present borrowers, on the same long-term basis. The banks would suffer loss of current income, but because of the greater safety of the credit, their regulators could permit them to schedule limited writedowns over a long period of time.

The political difficulties of such a program are immense. There would be a cry of "bailing out the banks," although the costs to the banks of such an approach would make it far from a bailout. A strong and healthy banking system is, in any case, vital to our own well-being. There would be opposition to easing credit abroad while American industry is in difficulties, even though the program would help increase American exports and actually create American jobs.

To make this approach work, coordinated Western growth is required, together with liberalized trade. That means that at a minimum Germany, France, Britain, Japan and the United States will have to agree on more expansive economic and monetary policies. In addition, a stabilization within realistic limits of the principal world trading currencies is a necessity.

Since the demise of the Bretton Woods exchange agreements in 1971, we have replaced a fixed-rate exchange system that had many problems but coincided with extraordinary growth with a floating-rate system that has even greater problems. The wild swings in currency rates, often caused by purely speculative movements of capital, have turned financial theories upside down. Instead of having trade patterns affect currency rates, these rates now affect trade patterns. The yen's weakness is ludicrous in light of Japanese exports flooding the world and domestic inflation of 5 percent. The automatic reaction to this is protectionism, no matter how counterproductive it may be in the end.

The time has come for much closer institutional ties among the main European currencies, the dollar and the yen. A 1983 version of the Bretton Woods conference could provide a framework for deciding among various options. These would include commitments by the central banks of the industrialized countries to maintain their currencies within agreed-upon ranges, coordination of monetary policies, possible expansion of the European monetary system to include the dollar and the yen, and expanded swap arrangements.

The present approach of insisting on IMF austerity programs while also keeping the borrowers under continuing crushing debt-service pressures could be self-defeating. Unless a strong—and unlikely—world-wide recovery occurs soon, the potential for social and political radicalization will increase, together with the risk of debt repudiation by one or more countries.

Other issues remain to be confronted. One difficult question: Should commercial banks lend to foreign governments on a long-term basis, or should this be handled on a government-to-government basis? I would argue that in the case of communist governments, such as the Soviet Union and those in Eastern Europe, these credits are of strategic value and should be handled government to government. They should become a part of our strategic negotiations with the Soviet Union. They have to be rolled over, and estimates are that an additional $40 billion to $50 billion of new credits will be needed over the next five years.

Together with our European allies, we should propose a long-term refinancing plan for Eastern Europe in which the Soviet Union would join us. It should provide half the credits and assume half the commitments. In the meantime, we should withhold rescheduling past debts, much less providing new credits.

If this means a bankruptcy of Poland, I would take it as an acceptable cost, and our respective central banks can ensure the viability of the banks involved. In a general sense, long-term loans are the province not of the banks but of insurance companies and the public markets.

The role of OPEC's more creditworthy members should also be expanded. Saudi Arabia, Kuwait and the Emirates should all have significant participation in the guarantees of credits, at a minimum. Their stake in the stability of the Western banking system is significant.

To sum up, the following requirements are basic to any long-term resolution of the current world debt problem:

- coordinated, aggressive economic growth policies among Western nations
- an orderly international monetary system whereby the main trading currencies are maintained within given ranges
- a long-term, low-interest refinancing of a significant part of the world debt
- maintenance of fair and liberal trade policies throughout the world

The economic summit to take place in May in Williamsburg, Virginia, could become the Bretton Woods conference of 1983. It provides a chance for the United States to take the leadership role that only we can play in the re-creation of a stable world-wide economic climate.

Business Week, February 28, 1983

A Letter to
Andrew Knight

Dear Andrew,

. . . I read, with great interest, your editorial "A Debt Partnership" in your issue of April 8 [, 1983]. I do not disagree with your recommendation. I wish, however, to clarify my own proposal since I believe that you have misunderstood it.

1. I do not advocate that an international agency *acquire* bank debt at a discount. That would require money from the markets to finance and would require banks to accept losses they may not wish to recognize.

I advocate the creation of an agency, guaranteed by the Western governments, which would *exchange* its own low-interest, long-term bonds for some of the banks' shorter-term, high-interest loans. The new agency would then turn those shorter-term, high-rate loans into mirror bonds* of the obligations it tendered to the banks.

Although the guarantees clearly involve the *possibility* of the commitment of public funds, none would be required at that time.

2. As far as the banks are concerned, they would have the following options:

a. They might refuse to participate in the exchange and continue to increase their exposure in the Third World through a series of short restructurings and additional loans to enable the borrowers to pay interest and meet minimal import needs; or

b. Exchange part of their loans for the new agency loans. Since these would be guaranteed, the banks would swap income

---

*"Mirror bonds" are bonds with similar maturities and interest rates to the bonds received in exchange.

for safety by accepting sharply lower interest rates and longer maturities for the increased safety of guarantees;

c. After the exchange, the banks could sell the guaranteed bonds on the public markets. Clearly, the bonds would sell at a considerable discount from par in view of their low rate of interest, but those banks with adequate loss reserves on their books now, could still sell the bonds without unacceptable accounting losses. This would create considerable liquidity for the banks wishing to avail themselves of that possibility;

d. The banks with low reserve positions would simply hold the guaranteed paper in lieu of their previous position. The regulators would clearly be more comfortable with the safer, although lower-yielding, long-term paper and should not require greater reserves. The depositors and stockholders should also feel reassured.

e. In view of the significant relief provided to the borrowers, the amount of new financing required from the banks should be reduced significantly. At the same time, the borrowers would be required to pay a guarantee fee of, say, 1 percent per annum and also be subjected to IMF scrutiny, as is presently the case;

f. Why is this not a "bailout for the banks"?

First, no Western government is going to let one of its major banks go down, no matter what.

Second, the taxpayers are partners with the banks, since loan losses are deductible for tax purposes.

Third, a 6 percent, twenty-five-year bond, fully guaranteed, is probably not worth much more than 50 percent of par in the marketplace. Therefore, a guarantee of such an instrument would be the equivalent, in real terms, of a 50 percent guarantee.

Fourth, the guarantee fee of 1 percent, over the life of the bond, would reduce this to, at most, 25 percent, and, in many cases, the guarantee would never be called upon.

g. The whole scheme could be tied to a formula based on a percentage of a country's exports so that acceleration of repayment would occur as commodity prices and exports rose;

h. Different terms could be set for different countries.

My only point in setting this forth to you is not because I want anything printed in *The Economist,* but because I should like you to understand what I have in mind. It is somewhat different from the Kenen proposal in that it requires no immediate cash. This problem is not going to go away, and I believe that our current approach to it is upside-down. The conventional wisdom is that recovery will solve this problem; my view is that we may never get recovery unless we solve the problem first. Recovery may be sufficient to enable borrowers barely to meet their debt service commitments. That is not enough. We need significant capacity, on the part of the Third World, to buy our goods, over and above debt service. I believe that a major increase in exports by the Organization for Economic Cooperation and Development (OECD) to the Third World is needed for recovery, since exports among OECD members will not be sufficient. Such an increase will require a major restructuring of the debt. I know that it is complicated and politically difficult, but once the will is there to do it, the mechanics will be found.

I also believe that it is likely that events will require such a restructuring. I think that, politically, we will be better off if we propose this to the Third World rather than doing it under the gun.

There are obviously many other approaches than the one I advocate that could accomplish the same objective. There has been some discussion about guaranteeing new credits, instead of old ones. That is clearly worth looking at. My main purpose in putting my suggestion forth was to encourage discussion, and to have some alternatives available in case things go awry.

In any case, thanks for taking the time to read this. I would much appreciate your views, hopefully in person, if you were to come over for Williamsburg. Incidentally, I believe the heads of state could appoint a group of, say, fifteen to twenty people, under the cochairmanship of Arthur Burns and Helmut Schmidt, to consider this problem along with exchange rates, and to come up with recommendations by year's end. They could then go back to the picture-taking, and have accomplished something at the same time . . .

Letter to Andrew Knight, April 21, 1983

The Case for Putting Poland in Default

WORLD EVENTS MAKE IT INCREASINGLY CLEAR THAT trade and credits will be a major element in our international posture—an essential strategic issue—toward the Soviet Union for the rest of the century. Like defense policy, our trade and credit policies toward the Soviet Union and Eastern Europe should be a systematic and integrated part of foreign policy, possibly subjected to regular if not annual congressional review and clearly linked to other East-West issues. The Polish situation provides a unique opportunity to develop such a strategy.

Three months after the imposition of martial law in Poland, however, what one finds is business as usual where American policy is concerned.

The New York *Times* on March 27, 1982, reported from Bonn that Poland appeared to have paid $500 million of overdue interest on its $2.4 billion of unpaid debt principal for 1981; the rescheduling of this amount is now taking place. At the same time, the report continued, talks will begin on rescheduling the 1982 debts, consisting of $10.4 billion of principal and interest.

It is not difficult to see where this is leading. The *Wall Street Journal* on March 15, 1982, quoted Jan Woloszyn, first deputy president of the Bank Handlowy, who stated that Poland would have to borrow the 1982 interest payments of $2.8 billion to $3 billion from Western banks. "We have to find credits from the West," he said. "If the banks want their money back, they will have to help us." In a *Wall Street Journal* interview later that month, the Polish deputy prime minister for industry, Janusz Obodowski, made it clear that Poland's willingness to meet its obligations to the West would depend on whether Western banks would provide new credits. The deputy foreign minister, Mr.

Rotowski, indicated that Poland would require $1.5 billion of new credit every quarter of 1982.

The next steps in this evolving negotiation are predictable. In the next few months, General Jaruzelski will lift martial law, having crushed Solidarity, and the Polish government will ask for new credits to restore its economy. It will agree to apply a small amount of these new credits to the currently overdue loans, and it will make pseudo-commitments of economic good behavior, such as application for membership in the International Monetary Fund. The Western banks and governments, after lengthy negotiations, will agree to the deal. Poland will be into the West for a larger amount, the Soviet Union will be relieved of the problem and the banks and governments will pretend they have good loans. This is bad foreign policy, bad business and bad morality. Poland should be put into default now as part of a coordinated Western plan.

The arguments against default—that it would endanger the Western banking system and upset our European allies who depend on trade with the East—do not withstand scrutiny.

The fact is that Poland is bankrupt, with no visible hope of meeting its future obligations without massive additional new debt.

To be viable, any new Polish credits would require the imposition of strict budgetary austerity, increased production quotas on coal and agriculture, longer work hours in factories, lower subsidies and higher prices; in short, rolling back many if not all of the economic benefits won by Solidarity would be a minimum requirement. But such controls are probably impossible to enforce, nor should Western banks and governments be put in the position of trying to impose them. The alternative is credit without controls, which hardly deserves comment.

Bankruptcy thus becomes self-evident.

What of the possible danger to Western banks? Of Poland's $25 billion of debt to Western banks and governments, a total of $1.2 billion is reportedly owed to U.S. banks, with the largest credits to individual banks in the area of $100 to $125 million. Our largest banks are well able to handle writeoffs of that size. But such writeoffs may not necessarily be required, and many banks must already have provided considerable reserves for such contingencies.

The real problem seems to be the German banks, where total exposure is said to be about $6 billion, of which 40 to 50 percent would be government-guaranteed, for a net exposure of $3 billion to $3.5 billion spread over 100 banks. The largest individual exposure seems to be of the order of $420 million, of which $340 million would be without guarantees.

Consider the reality of this situation. Banking problems occur in two areas: liquidity and net capital. One is a matter of cash, the other of accounting. The German banks clearly have no liquidity problem, since the Polish loans are paying interest late and paying no principal at all; furthermore, any potential liquidity problem can be handled easily by the German central bank, just as equivalent problems can be handled by the Federal Reserve Bank here.

What is involved here is net capital, or what are essentially accounting problems. Large writeoffs or additional reserves would reduce the banks' stated capital, reduce reported earnings and possibly reduce or eliminate dividends for some time. But the Polish loans already are bad loans; declaring Poland in default will not make them worse. Accounting fictions should not dictate foreign policy.

It is claimed that the threat of default creates greater pressures than its actual imposition because of the current payment of interest. But if this be true, why is Poland so desperately trying to avoid default? Why doesn't Poland simply declare itself in default on its own, which it could easily do? The answer is that interest payments are a small price to pay to keep Western financial institutions interested in Poland's future, maintaining the illusion of Polish creditworthiness and continuing the conflict between the West's short-term commercial interests and its long-term geopolitical interest.

Another argument against a Polish default is that the effects of default have already appeared in the sharp curtailment of credit to Eastern Europe. But the dynamics of the present situation inevitably lead to new commercial credits to protect the old ones. These will not create a stable long-term trade climate; they simply increase Western exposure.

Intellectually the least plausible argument goes to the issue of "friendship with the Polish people." A decade of détente and $25 billion of Western credits have not moved Poland out of the Soviet orbit; that should have taught us something.

What, then, does logic dictate?

The availability of large-scale credit facilities is a strategic weapon, the one major item the United States can withhold which the Soviet Union cannot obtain elsewhere, especially in a world increasingly short of capital.

The *Wall Street Journal,* using Wharton economic forecasts, estimated recently that the Soviet bloc's requirements for dollar credit would increase from about $70 billion at the end of 1980 to as much as $140 billion by 1985. The Soviet Union has been selling gold, diamonds and oil to raise foreign exchange and asking its Western suppliers for extended credit terms. The Soviet bloc's additional external requirement of $70 billion will have to be met by retrenchment somewhere else (possibly armaments), or by a recognition that accommodation with the West is preferable to continuing the arms race.

All this points to the notion that credits to Eastern Europe should be handled on a government-to-government basis through central banks as part of our strategic dialogue with the Soviet Union. Banking transactions should be limited to self-liquidating commercial transactions and should not include long-term loans to Soviet bloc governments. Furthermore, it would seem reasonable to suggest that we provide new credits to the Soviet bloc only as part of overall negotiations with the Soviet Union and as participants in an economic recovery plan for Eastern Europe to which the Soviet Union would contribute at a minimum, say, twice what we contribute.

To set the stage, the existing Polish debt in the hands of commercial banks should be acquired by their respective central banks at some discount from the face amount, say 50 percent, with final determination deferred until a plan of reorganization is worked out with the creditor state or states. The banks would get immediate cash, which would improve their liquidity. They could then take tax credits in recognition of the loss. To the extent their balance sheets required it, they could be permitted to defer some of their losses until a final accounting takes place. That would solve the bank problem and provide our Western allies with necessary assurances as to the underpinnings of the banking system. This plan is not without cost, but these loans were never without risk. The Western governments could then, on a coordinated basis, declare Poland in default and cut off additional credits to Eastern Europe.

Simultaneously, the West could offer to participate in Soviet efforts to refinance Eastern Europe, but only if such refinancing were linked to other matters under negotiation now. According to recent reports, the Soviet economy is becoming increasingly strapped at a time of world-wide economic contraction, capital shortages and falling prices for oil, diamonds and gold, the Russians' biggest sources of foreign exchange. The Soviet Union may find accommodation with the West the best of many unpleasant alternatives.

For our European allies, our offer to negotiate a long-term economic assistance plan between West and East would tangibly recognize their trade needs. Only such a plan would put East-West trade on a sound footing without jeopardizing Western interests. We should offer parallel negotiations, offering arms control on the one hand and economic development on the other.

In any case, we have little to lose by playing the hand out slowly. Soon after Poland will come Romania, then Hungary. The West can sit and wait, offering to cooperate but at a price and on our terms. The balance of power will have been shifted; sooner or later there will be a negotiation.

The prize is very large, the potential benefits to the West significant. Forgoing some interest payments and losing loans that will never be repaid seem a small price to pay for a dramatic change in our posture in relation to Russia. The Soviet Union should be challenged to join the West in diverting investments from weapons to more productive uses. It will be a tough, hard road, but the prize is worth the cost. The starting point is a Polish default.

The *Wall Street Journal,* April 19, 1982

Chapter Three

———— ટ✦ ————————————————————

A COMMENCEMENT ADDRESS IS DIFFERENT FROM ANY
other kind of speech. It should deal with fundamental issues
instead of the arcane mysteries of fiscal and monetary policies.
As a result, I have found such addresses to be possibly more
educational for me than for my audience. I gave this speech at
my alma mater, Middlebury College, in 1982, when we were in
deep recession.

The theme that I attempted to illustrate was the transitional
nature of American society and the need for flexibility in
government to cope with it. I am still convinced that there has
to be a middle road between the liberalism of the 1960s and the
Reaganism or Thatcherism of the 1980s. I am very much aware
of the appearance of "wishy-washiness" of any middle-of-the-
road position set against the apparent hard edges and clean
lines of the present conservatism.

But we live in a disorderly, complicated, rapidly changing
world. I do not believe that our most important problems will
respond to simple, totally market-oriented, hands-off solutions.
Neither will our race problems, industrial problems,
educational problems, regional problems or urban problems
respond to such simplicities. They require a government
willing to intervene and business and labor willing to
cooperate.

In this commencement address I also alluded to my greatest
fear, the fear for our political institutions if we cannot cope
with our problems. We have tried liberalism; we are now trying
conservatism. If we continue to be frustrated by the results,

this could lead to political experiments much more extreme than anything we have witnessed so far. I do not care to witness such experiments.

Commencement

IT HAS BEEN MORE THAN THIRTY YEARS SINCE I GRAD-
uated, without the slightest distinction, from a small, idyllic, some
might say ivory tower, college in Vermont called Middlebury. I
had come to the United States in 1942, a refugee from Nazi-
occupied France. America meant freedom and opportunity for me;
Franklin Roosevelt was America. Middlebury was part of a heady
postwar period, of belonging somewhere, of becoming a U.S. citi-
zen, of having a future. A small, bouncy, bald professor named
Benjamin Wissler taught me the difference between a fact and an
assumption, between reasoning and guessing. Even though soon
after graduation I was drafted for the Korean War and graduated
from that experience as a sergeant of infantry, also without distinction, nothing during that period dimmed my conviction that in the
United States, tomorrow would be better than today, as would
every tomorrow thereafter. Insofar as I am concerned, America
has far exceeded my personal expectations. No European country
would have given a Jewish refugee of Polish extraction the opportunities in business and in public affairs that this country has given
me.

And yet it would be disingenuous and unrealistic not to recognize that the world as a whole and the United States in particular
are profoundly changed since my graduating year of 1949.

A friend of mine, one of the more civilized corporate chairmen,
said to me recently: "I no longer give commencement addresses;
the graduates are entitled to an upbeat speech, and I am no longer
capable of delivering one." That gave me pause because I certainly
do not have an upbeat speech; however, a realistic assessment of
where we are cannot be equated with hopelessness. We saved New
York City from bankruptcy against much greater odds than those

facing this country today. But we did it by being ruthlessly realistic about the mess we were dealing with and by assuming, quite correctly, that when things look very bad, they usually turn out to be worse than they look.

The United States and the world as a whole are messy, but they are better than they were. They have always been messy, for that is the nature of most societies, but things are clearly no worse today than they were in the 1930s, with a worldwide depression and with Hitler and Stalin to deal with. In earlier times, tsarist Russia, nineteenth-century England and eighteenth-century France were not exactly lands of opportunity for most of their citizens. Today we are facing some highly complicated, possibly intractable problems on a very large scale all over the world. We have at our disposal exploding levels of technology as well as instantaneous and almost infinite access to information. As a result, the United States today faces an uncertain but certainly not hopeless future. Unfortunately, it faces this future with an ideology and a philosophy more suitable to the past than to the present.

After our most recent presidential election, the nation was mesmerized first by the theory and then by the implementation of supply-side economics, a program that turned out to be based on the theory of John Maynard Keynes in disguise. After all, running large deficits as a result of tax cuts and defense spending is little different in an economic sense from running large deficits as a result of social programs and public works. Either way the country eventually goes bankrupt. However, while everyone's attention was focused on President Reagan's economic program, few of us paid attention to President Reagan's truly radical initiative, namely the deliberate use of huge deficits to bludgeon the Congress into reducing dramatically the role, and the responsibility, of government.

The American Revolution of 1981 was, therefore, as profound in its reach as it was little noticed in its underlying philosophy. The last fifty years have witnessed a basic continuity on the part of one Administration after another on two counts: first, that government had a responsibility to improve the lot of those unable to help themselves; second, that the American free enterprise system could not rely solely on the free market to provide opportunity for all of our people. Even President Nixon, when forced by events, imposed wage and price controls and enacted sweeping environmental legislation, as well as revenue-sharing, in support of this philosophy. The Revolution of 1981 is changing all that. The United States today is more than a nation; it is a continent. Within this continent lie our greatest challenges and the most serious threats to our democratic form of government: income and class disparities on the one hand, regional disparities on the other. The Reagan Administration's approach to these issues was to state that tax policy should not be used to effect social change and that citizens should vote with their feet, by moving from our distressed regions to our wealthier ones.

This approach has led to a budget and tax policy that not only reversed fifty years of attempts to reduce disparities, but will actually and quite considerably increase them. A completely laudable attempt to improve American productivity by stimulating investment has resulted in an economic program incoherent in its application. Corporate income taxes and high income brackets have been reduced significantly, while at the lower end of the income scale Americans have seen their modest tax cuts more than offset by budget cuts and their financial security devastated by recession.

Budget cuts have been largely concentrated on lower-income programs such as food stamps, welfare and Medicaid, and have not, so far, touched the large middle-income support programs indexed to the cost of living, such as Social Security, Medicare and pensions. Massive tax cuts, coupled with enormous and apparently indiscriminate increases in military spending, have created the prospect of enormous federal deficits for years to come. The growth in the economy which was expected to pay for these programs is, time and again, choked off by the high interest rates resulting from a tight monetary policy and the expectation of huge government borrowing.

At the same time, a strong regional tide is running away from this part of the country. Unless vigorous actions are taken soon (assuming that it is not already too late), the younger, better educated, more highly skilled, upper-income white Americans will concentrate themselves in the Sunbelt. Attracted by a pleasant life-style, lower taxes and career opportunities in energy, defense and high-technology industries, they will leave the Northeast and Midwest to those less fortunate. Older America, tied to traditional industries like autos, steel, glass and rubber, seriously wounded by Japanese competition, will not provide the jobs, the schools or the tax base to maintain the physical plant of its cities and the minimum requirements of its citizens. Half of this country will be basking in the sun, amply supplied with oil and defense contracts, while the other half will sink further and further into physical decay, social stress and despair.

Perhaps for the first time in our history, large numbers of Americans are worried about their destiny. In as few as twenty years we have gone from the American Century to the American Crisis. From having a nuclear monopoly and absolute military superiority on earth, we have seen our monopoly shattered and our superiority reduced to doubtful parity with the Soviet Union. Our currency and our gold reserves have been steadily eroded by domestic inflation and reduced international competitiveness. A deep-seated American conviction that our children's future would be brighter than ours, that our ability to produce and create wealth knew no limits and that all Americans would ultimately share in this cornucopia, has given way to doubt. Neither we nor our children believe that they will be better off than we were; we are now extremely conscious of the limit of our resources and of the need to cut back on some activities; the opportunities open to many Americans are being sharply curtailed.

The sine qua non of a functioning democracy is its ability to create new wealth and see to its fair distribution. The tides now running in this country are likely to do just the opposite. Wealth will be created for too few; too many will be left behind. The question of fairness will come up again and again, especially if economic growth remains anemic. When a democratic society does not meet the test of fairness—when, as is now the case, the Administration seems indifferent to fairness—freedom is in jeopardy.

A great danger facing modern democracy is the difficulty of allocating sacrifice fairly. But a growing economy allows even an arthritic political system to apportion some of that growth to all elements of society, something that cannot happen in a stagnating economy. Where sacrifice has to be apportioned, single-interest groups take savage retribution on any politician reckless enough to challenge them. Whether the issue be Social Security, defense installations or gasoline prices, enough contrary votes can always be mobilized to exercise veto power.

We have seen in 1981 that legislating sacrifice puts the burden on those least able to afford it, while moderating inflation can come only through the bitter medicine of steep recession. Those solutions are neither fair nor likely, ultimately, to be effective. At a time of stress, all members of society must share the burden. Sacrifice has to be negotiated, not legislated. These negotiations must take place in a variety of forums, and the government must be willing and eager to take its place at the negotiating table along with business and labor. I am suggesting not a super State to superimpose itself on normal democratic procedures, but a process of continued negotiation to set the goals and limits within which the United States can achieve its necessary objectives: stable, continued economic private-sector growth and fairness in the distribution of new wealth among classes and regions. For me, the lesson of the near bankruptcy of New York City suggests that this could be done on a national scale.

The United States today is in transition from being the world's dominant military power to sharing that role with the Soviet Union; from being an industrial to a service society; from being a predominantly white, northern European society based in the Northeast and Midwest to being a multiracial society with its center of gravity in the Sunbelt. A society in transition cannot be governed by rigid dogma. It requires a government that is flexible, pragmatic, even sometimes deliberately ambiguous. Shared values must be clear, but the means to the end cannot be rigid. From fascism to communism, from monarchy to anarchy, the ends of government are purportedly the same: justice with opportunity, higher standard of living, peace in our time. The means to the ends are very different, however, and the means are what determine whether or not we live in a free society.

The critical issues we face today are not the levels of interest rates or what kind of package finally comes out of budget negotiations. These things are important, but our fascination with numbers must not obscure the real issues. These are, in no particular order:

- the rapid growth of a permanent underclass in America: the residents of inner-city ghettos, black and Hispanic, undereducated, underskilled, without real hope of participating in the future of the country
- the regional split between Sunbelt and Frostbelt, which is accelerating and which will leave the northern half of the United States in serious difficulty
- the decline of our traditional manufacturing sectors (autos, steel, glass, rubber) and the automation which will create long-term employment in the hardest-hit part of the country
- the illusion that we have resolved our energy problems
- illegal immigration in great numbers, especially from Mexico, which will create additional social tensions unless we produce enough jobs to absorb our own unemployed along with new arrivals
- nuclear proliferation and the need to control and reduce the level of nuclear weapons while being realistic about Soviet power
- the decay of our cities and the decline in the quality of urban life
- the decline of the written press and the dominance of TV in the political dialogue of the nation
- the roller-coaster economy which knows only inflation or recession, or both, but seems unable to produce stable noninflationary growth
- the mountains of debt crushing every level of society (individual corporations, as well as local and federal governments)

To be fair, I should not ignore the many reasons today for optimism: the new technologies, the exploration of space and of the oceans, new systems of communication and advances in medicine and knowledge of the body.

If I dwell on the problems, it is for two reasons: first, because I have been trained, professionally, to look after the bad news first and let the good news take care of itself; second, because I believe that in our problems lie the opportunities for tomorrow.

And yet the problems that I have reviewed are by no means the complete list. Furthermore, their diversity and complexity indicate the hopelessness of trying to deal with them by across-the-board economic theories and "hands-off" government. The role of government in the last decades of this century will be the paramount question facing our citizens.

Today we are witnessing a paradox: a government that abdicates to a theoretical marketplace most of its responsibilities for the welfare of the people, while wishing to intrude on people's most private decisions. How does one equate the conservative passion to intrude on such issues as abortion and school prayer with the voters' fervent claim that the free market is the source of all benefits? Today's conservative experiment will fail because it is not relevant to the world we live in, just as yesterday's liberalism failed for the same reason. We are soon, however, going to run out of time for experiments.

Benny Wissler once snappily explained to me that there was no such thing as *the wrong answer*; there was only *a wrong answer,* one among many.

It was only recently, however, that I concluded that, especially in government and public life, there may not be *a right answer.* Perhaps at best there is only a process whereby we can modify trends and temporarily influence the direction of social and economic behavior. I am skeptical of planned, centralized government, but I do think government should anticipate destabilizing trends before they become floodtides—a permanent but ever-changing process.

A Rabelaisian friend once compared saving New York City to making love to a gorilla. "You don't stop when you're tired," he said to me, "you stop when he's tired." The gorilla never tires and government can never abdicate its responsibilities.

We must recognize, however, that it was the unrealistic bureaucratic liberalism of the Great Society and the perceived wishy-washiness of the Carter Administration that brought us the Reagan Revolution. We may be heading for an economic and social catastrophe with supply-side economics and the Laffer curve; we were surely headed for one with runaway spending, runaway inflation and the appearance of weakness symbolized by the Iranian hostage crisis.

What alternatives are we facing if President Reagan's social and economic experiment fails?

One rather frightening scenario described by Kevin Phillips in a recent article entitled "Post-Reagan America"* involves far greater government control over the economy stimulated by authoritarian right-wing populism, limiting political and social dissent in the name of law and order. To those who say it cannot happen here, I would simply say that democracy is a fragile system and we are stretching it to the breaking point. The essential questions of fairness and opportunity cannot be answered in the affirmative today by an economic policy that seems to favor the wealthy and a government that invests mostly in the military.

Another scenario is scarcely more inspiring. The shrill and sometimes violent attacks on many of our institutions by liberals of the late 1960s and early 1970s created the impression among millions of Americans that liberalism was opposed to such basic values as love of country, love of family, and the work ethic. While this was happening, many of the Great Society social programs, enacted in the 1960s for perfectly valid reasons, led to uncontrollable spending and threatened to bankrupt our economy. The problem of liberalism in a world of limited resources is its tendency to submit to pressures for excessive spending. A bankrupt country cannot sustain a free people. Meanwhile, the liberal zeal for political reform so weakened our political parties that they have been largely replaced by the financial power of political action committees and the activities of special-interest lobbyists. We are paying the price of such "reform."

Where can we go, then, if neither conservatism nor liberalism has the answers and if Jimmy Carter's failed attempt to find a middle ground proves to be typical of such efforts? Recently the head of the French Socialist Party compared the political center to the Bermuda Triangle. "Everyone who goes there, disappears forever," he said. And yet the answers, if there are any, must come from a rational middle ground; however, it need not be wishy-washy.

There is no reason that a hard-headed liberalism cannot live with the reality that we cannot spend ourselves into bankruptcy.

There is no reason that social programs, impeccable in their objectives, have to be grossly expanded to include those who really don't need them.

*New York Review of Books, May 13, 1982.

There is no reason that an economy geared mostly to private-sector growth cannot at the same time permit limited government intervention where it is needed. A modern version of the Reconstruction Finance Corporation of the 1930s could help rebuild our cities and restructure our basic industries without threatening our basic free-enterprise system.

There is no reason that limited and temporary protection for our hard-hit industries cannot be conditioned on restrained wage and price behavior by labor and management, conditions that might become the model for an incomes policy where wages and prices are linked to productivity.

There is no reason that savings and investment cannot be encouraged while energy use and other forms of consumption are taxed at higher rates, to produce growth and jobs. Some of these jobs could be directed, with government assistance but under private-sector management, to inner-city ghettos to provide a future where none currently exists.

There is no reason that large savings cannot be effected in defense, and particularly in reducing nuclear delivery systems, if we are willing to pay the price of larger standing conventional forces and the distasteful possibility of a peacetime draft.

There is no reason to abandon human rights abroad and tolerate murderers from the right because they happen to be anticommunist. Nor is there reason to tolerate murderers from the left on the romantic notion that they are agrarian reformers.

But while there is no intrinsic reason that all these results cannot be achieved, we must be realistic about the political difficulties of bringing them about. Without the active support of the American people and the active cooperation of business, labor and government, they cannot happen.

In times of upheaval, the passions must be for moderation and not for extremes. As Anwar Sadat well knew, the passion for moderation can be dangerous, and yet it is absolutely vital to our future. Sadat took the risks, and paid the price. Even though today's technology provides us with mountains of instant data, it is useless without judgment. And if judgments are to have value, policy decisions have to be made early, when the magnitude of the problem is only dimly perceived, but when there is still latitude for action; when the crisis is clear, it is often too late to act. That is the dilemma of statesmanship and the possibly fatal flaw in a political process that can act only when it is too late.

France has given the world a lot, not least the skepticism of Montaigne and of Voltaire. Skepticism is what is needed today— skepticism of easy solutions, of cant, of ideology of the left or right. Skepticism is not cynicism; it is not inconsistent with the fiercest patriotism or the firmest belief in basic values. But it can be the anchor to windward when our basic institutions seem to be adrift. There is little stability in a system where the President begins to run for reelection after a year or two in office, where congressmen are constantly running, where political theories as well as politicians are peddled like soap on TV commercials with the caveat that, with politicians, as opposed to soap, you cannot return what you have bought because it does not perform.

Politics is not the only way to become involved in public life. There will be many structures such as the Municipal Assistance Corporation, where private citizens can play important roles. Everyone has his heroes; one of mine is Jean Monnet. A French bourgeois, whose family owned a famous cognac, Jean Monnet changed the political and economic face of postwar Europe without once serving in a French administration. He was the author of the European Coal and Steel Authority, which then led to the creation of the European Common Market. Monnet played the roles of negotiator, agitator, propagandist, tactician and strategist, which are needed to effect fundamental political change in a democratic society. Mao Tse-tung believed that power for change grew out of the barrel of a gun; Monnet believed that power for change grew out of the acts of economic institutions.

I had the privilege of participating in a great adventure, the rescue of New York City. It was an experience both terrifying and exhilarating, which I would not have missed for anything. It taught me what you will find out: to be skeptical and always look over your shoulder, but to get involved deeply and to shoot for the moon; to beware of lawyers and consultants and people who do not take risks and who do not get their hands dirty. There are even more experts today than there are problems, but there is no greater strength than an open mind combined with a willingness to take risks. Middlebury opened my mind as I am sure it did yours. In order to take risks, however, you have to go in harm's way. What happens then, and how you perform, will depend on the fates as well as on your character.

Commencement address, Middlebury College,
Middlebury, Vermont, May 23, 1982

Chapter Four

PRESIDENT REAGAN'S SECOND STATE OF THE UNION
message in January 1982 brought forth a proposal for a New
Federalism. Although I believe there is much merit in
reordering some state/federal relationships, his proposal seemed
fraught with dangers. I discussed this in the *New York Review
of Books* in April 1982.

The New Federalism initiative, in its original form,
disappeared from the political agenda because it was deeply
flawed; as proposed, it was really a vehicle to transfer more
deficits from the federal government to local governments. This
is unfortunate because, if properly conceived, it could have a
very positive impact.

A New Federalism could do much to bring economic
recovery to the hardest-hit parts of the country by encouraging
local tax reductions. A suggestion for such an approach is
contained in this essay.

Though it has disappeared from the political dialogue, a
New Federalism, properly conceived, could be enormously
beneficial in helping to provide economic growth and regional
balance, both of which are sorely needed.

At the time of this writing the 1983 economic recovery has
reduced some of the pressures alluded to in this article, and the
social unrest I had been fearful of has not come about.
However, I believe the fundamental premise is still valid. The
local tax increases I had predicted for the northeastern and
midwestern states have largely come about, the need for

cooperation by the President and Congress to face up to our deficits still exists and the employment and urban problems of vast parts of the country are largely unimproved.

A Raw Deal

APRIL 1982

PRESIDENT REAGAN'S CALL FOR A "NEW FEDERALISM" deserves better than automatic praise by Republicans and equally reflexive criticism by Democrats. State/federal relations have been a subject of concern to local officials for years, and a national program to sort out those relationships is overdue. The fact that the Administration's program appears to have serious flaws should not detract from the fact that there is a need for change. It does, however, mean that serious, dispassionate examination should be made of the program.

Any proposal as far-reaching as President Reagan's obviously starts off with the inertia of the status quo working against it. Its chances for success or failure will depend as much on the timing of the proposal as on its substance. And the timing is very bad indeed. The dismal performance of the economy, together with last year's tax and budget cuts, has created enormous fiscal pressures on local governments in practically all but the energy-producing regions of the country. The state of Ohio, which recently passed a tax increase of $1.3 billion together with expenditure cuts to close its budget gap, now faces an additional deficit of about $1 billion as a result of the recession.

New York City, with a $250 million surplus in the current fiscal year, is raising taxes and freezing employment to deal with a potential $800 million gap next year. The state of New York is proposing similar actions for the same reason. Whereas four years ago the Municipal Assistance Corporation was selling long-term bonds to finance New York City's capital budget at 7.5 percent interest, it is doing so today, with increasing difficulty, at over 14 percent, free of city, state and federal income taxes. This situation is repeated in city after city, state after state.

This is not happening only in the Frostbelt while the Sunbelt flourishes. The state of California now faces a budget deficit estimated at $1 billion. A recent New York *Times* article noted that many cities in the Sunbelt suffer as much from unemployment, poor housing, poverty and limited economic opportunities as the cities in the Northeast and Midwest. Of nineteen Sunbelt cities, seven had worse hardship ratings than New York. The Sunbelt's golden glow cannot hide the difficulties faced by New Orleans, Miami, Birmingham, Atlanta and other cities within its midst. Their problems are national.

Long-term policy changes, such as those currently advocated by the Reagan Administration, require a stable economic base from which data can be extrapolated in order for rational dialogue on federal-state relations to take place. Until we have a better fix on the recovery of the economy and federal deficits, on inflation and interest rates, it will be utterly impossible for local officials struggling with serious day-to-day fiscal problems to project with any confidence their own set of numbers. Until the economy stabilizes, it will not really be possible to have negotiations of any substance. As Governor James Hunt of North Carolina said, "We want the nation's economic problems addressed first."

What is needed today is a summit meeting, involving the President, the congressional leadership and the chairman of the Federal Reserve Bank, that will try to resolve the budget impasse and to permit an easing of monetary policy and interest rates. But if such a meeting produced an agreement, it still would not solve our long-term economic dislocations; that is an illusion that should be dispelled. Budget and interest rate problems need to be solved first to avoid economic disaster. Only then can we take up the issue of federalism along with our many other dilemmas.

How can midwestern states look at their future unemployment costs without some notion of where the automotive industry's domestic production will ultimately stabilize? Indeed, how can any state even begin to judge its taxing capacity five to ten years from now, and its ability to take over those programs suggested by the President, without knowing how much of its local taxing power will be required to make up for cuts transferred to local governments currently and to make up for the current recession's revenue loss?

Until the economy stabilizes, the President has written a symphony for a deaf audience; local officials will hear only the day-to-day problems of their own constituents and argue, with some logic, that in order to solve tomorrow's problems we have to survive today's. A more serious timing problem could result if state legislatures, faced with very difficult decisions, find an excuse for inaction in the expectation of the New Federalism. The New York state legislature is about to consider a politically difficult program involving the takeover of the local share of Medicaid, to be financed by various tax increases. Despite a sensible alternative proposal to consider an interim, one-year takeover program, the legislature may well use the supposed coming of the New Federalism as an excuse to defer any action. That would have disastrous effects in both the cities and counties.

It seems virtually impossible, in view of the upcoming battle in Congress over the budget, which will have great impact on the fiscal capacity of many states, that a national debate on the New Federalism can take place this year. To the question of "If not now, when?" the answer could well be "Same time, next year."

Let us now consider Reagan's federalism proposal itself. It consists of two parts.

First, it proposes a swap of Medicaid costs for state assumption of the costs of welfare and food stamps. The Administration estimates that federal payment of all Medicaid costs would save the states $19.1 billion in fiscal 1984, while the assumption of welfare and food stamp programs by the states would cost them $16.5 billion, for a net gain of $2.6 billion.

Second, the President makes a separate proposal to turn back to the states full responsibility for a variety of current federal programs, including transportation, revenue-sharing, education and community economic development. The Administration has not yet published a complete list of the programs it intends to turn back, so it is impossible to estimate the costs of this proposal with certainty. The Administration claims that these costs would be offset—at least initially—by savings from the swap and from a temporary federalism trust fund of $28 billion from the windfall profits tax on oil and other excise taxes.

Overall, the Administration estimates that the program would be financially harmless to the states, so that no state would suffer an increased burden in the initial stages of the program. This optimistic claim is possible only if one accepts the Administration's proposals for further cuts in Aid for Families with Dependent Children (AFDC) and food stamps—cuts that Congress seems increasingly less willing to make. When the Congressional Budget Office estimated the effect of swapping the costs of Medicaid for the costs of AFDC and food stamps in 1981, it concluded that the states would lose $4.4 billion. If the swap were made in 1984 without changes in the current policy, the budget office estimated a shortfall to the states of $1.5 billion (compared to the Administration's estimated gain of $2.6 billion).

For the program as a whole, the Congressional Budget Office has concluded that in 1984 the shortfall to the states for both the swap and turnback/trust-fund program would be $15 billion. The most serious financial problem would come as the trust fund is phased out between 1987 and 1991. At that point, the states would have the choice of either dropping these programs or imposing some equivalent of the windfall profits tax on oil and other federal excise taxes. Obviously, imposing a windfall profits tax on oil is not feasible for any but the country's energy-producing states; for the rest, the Reagan plan is merely a formula for assuring the elimination of programs or increases in local taxes. This is bad medicine not only for the states, but for the country.

Any debate on federalism should, I think, be based on two principles. First, government programs should be operated by state and local governments if these have established their own competence to run them—for example, in education and transportation—and if state-by-state differences in programs and program levels are not unfair. Americans have never believed that all prerogatives are local. Should the poor and the elderly receive different medical care solely because they live in richer or poorer states? Second, no matter who runs programs, they should be paid for fairly. Our personal-income-tax system, for all its shortcomings, is well run and based on the principle of ability to pay. Why should support for education, economic development or job-training programs be any different?

The inevitable result of the Administration's turnback would be to increase reliance on the most unpopular and unfairly based tax of all: the property tax. A community's ability to provide services would be the chance result of its local tax base. For some services, such as education, the results of this approach have been found unconstitutional; in other cases they are merely unfair and unwise. More than a decade ago, another Republican President, Richard Nixon, recognized this principle and established revenue-sharing of federal tax receipts with the states and cities. Under revenue-sharing, locally run programs were supported by the fairer and more efficient federal tax system. It is unfortunate that the current version of the New Federalism ignores this system. This is one of the program's major deficiencies.

A little-noticed but important result of the current national economic experiment is that it has acted as a powerful force for local tax increases. The federal government, in its pursuit of budget cuts and its inability, so far, to stimulate the economy, has brought an avalanche of deficits down on state and local governments unable to absorb them. The deficits following initiatives such as Proposition 13 have required many states and municipalities to seek tax increases while cutting their own budgets. A survey of cities conducted by the Joint Economic Committee of Congress found that over 40 percent of those who responded (of which half were cities with unemployment over 10 percent) had raised their tax rates. This fiscal pressure creates a further drag on the economy, slows recovery and reduces federal tax receipts due to the deductibility of local taxes.

Any program of national recovery that reshuffles federal and state responsibilities must create an incentive to reduce local taxes as opposed to increasing them. Such reductions would provide considerable stimulus to the economy, especially in those states hard hit by recession and foreign competition.

From these considerations, we could develop a somewhat different proposal: a New Federalism that would continue to assign to the federal government all income-transfer programs related to poverty and would switch to the states the remaining programs proposed by the President. Medicaid, food stamps and welfare would remain federal responsibilities, administered nationally with national standards. The states would be relieved of Medicaid, a program that is estimated to cost $19.1 billion in 1984 and is growing rapidly. The programs to be turned back to the states are estimated to cost $30 to $44 billion by 1984, depending upon whose figures you accept. For this plan to have a neutral fiscal impact, it would be necessary to transfer a stable and permanent revenue source to the states, such as a portion of sharply increased gasoline taxes.

I have advocated for some time an increase of fifty cents per gallon in gasoline taxes both to close our budget gap (and thereby bring down interest rates) and to put greater pressure on OPEC prices and reduce our energy consumption still further. There could be no better time for such a tax than when oil prices are going down, as they are now. Of the $50 billion annually raised by such a tax increase, a portion could be transferred to the states to finance these programs. A combination of gasoline taxes and import fees on crude oil would be another possibility. Ultimately, the fairest means of raising revenues would be one suggested recently by *Business Week,* namely to "dampen down regional and state rivalries by imposing a federal tax on energy resources with the revenues being distributed to all states through a revenue-sharing program." No such federal severance tax is likely to be enacted soon.

Once the states have assumed responsibility for these programs, we should require that any reductions in them be accompanied by equivalent local tax reductions. Similarly, we should require local tax reductions in every state where the net effect of the national program is to decrease state obligations. If the Administration is serious about wanting a smaller federal government, more local responsibility and fairness in the distribution of burdens and benefits, such an approach would have obvious advantages. Local tax reductions would be a larger political incentive for states to drop useless programs, and the federal government would share in the benefit as a result of the overall economic stimulus such tax cuts might produce.

Such a proposal differs from the Administration's in two ways. First, it would keep poverty programs under federal control. There is no reasonable case for splitting Medicare from Medicaid. Likewise, AFDC and food stamps should remain national responsibilities—everyone eligible for AFDC and many eligible for food stamps also receive Medicaid.

Second, it would support local programs from the national tax base and yet permit local taxes to be reduced. Many critics of the

Administration believe the federalism proposal is nothing more than a clever attempt to subtract $30 billion in federal programs from the budget by offering a temporary trust fund and the carrot of taking over the state contributions to Medicaid. I hope the Administration is sincere, but no program will succeed that offers the states only the painful choice of—and the accompanying blame for—either killing programs or raising taxes.

No discussion of the "New Federalism" can ignore the issues of disparities and major imbalances that are beginning to build serious pressures in this country. Everywhere one turns, disparities are getting greater, not smaller.

Consider regional disparities. A recent survey of the National Conference of State Legislatures found that thirty-nine states were facing deficits for the current fiscal year or municipal surpluses below necessary safeguards. The states with the most serious budgetary problems were Washington, Minnesota, Massachusetts, Michigan, Ohio, Oregon, Kentucky and California. The seven states (apart from Alaska, which is in a class by itself) with the largest surpluses were Oklahoma, Texas, Wyoming, Nevada, New Mexico, Kansas and North Dakota, all of them energy-producing states.

The same story is also occurring in the cities. The survey of cities by the Joint Economic Committee that I mentioned earlier found widespread plans for service cuts. Fifty-six percent of those who responded admitted to plans for deferring capital spending on water supply and sewers, streets, building maintenance, etc. At the same time, the Northeast and Midwest, with 47 percent of our population, receive 35 percent of defense funds and 20 percent of defense jobs. The South and West, which account for 51 percent of the population, are getting 64 percent of defense funds and 79 percent of defense jobs. It should be easy to see what the dynamics of energy, defense and sunshine are doing to the distribution of wealth in the United States.

While this is happening, the Reagan Administration's budget and tax policy is increasing the disparity between the well-to-do and the poor. By 1985 the net positive impact of federal budget and tax policy on households having more than $48,000 in annual income will be $140 billion; on households with annual income of $11,500 the net effect will be minus $24 billion. The proposed 1983 budget, for instance, would cut programs for the poor such as child nutrition, Medicaid and welfare by 10 to 18 percent, while programs of essentially middle-class income support such as Social Security, pensions and Medicare are cut from 0 to 4 percent. According to the House Budget Committee, 60 percent of the Administration's proposals to reduce the deficit in fiscal 1983 would cut programs to assist the poor and disadvantaged; yet these programs will represent only 6 percent of all federal spending. In the meantime, defense spending will go up by 18 percent. What we are witnessing is not only a high-risk economic program but a radical reordering of our social structures. A functioning democracy must be perceived as attempting to be fair. None of these policies meets the elemental test of fairness.

Everywhere we look, we find that this process of creating more acute social imbalances is accelerating: industrial unemployment in the Midwest as a result of Japanese competition and recession; taxpayer migration from the Northeast as a result of the attraction of Sunbelt regions able to lower taxes and increase services. Superimposed on this process is a steep recession brought on by the collision of huge budgetary deficits with restrictive monetary policy, with high interest rates as a result. The currently lower rate of inflation has been achieved by paying the price of high and rising unemployment and dangerously deteriorating financial structures. But behind the dry statistics of the economists, one finds growing misery and despair among millions who cannot find work and untold others who have given up trying. Violence is the companion of despair. It does not take a soothsayer or an alarmist to predict that, if this process continues into the summer, it may be a very hot summer indeed. We have become dangerously complacent about what can happen when over 60 percent of young blacks in Wayne County, Michigan, are unemployed and when a sizable portion of our population believes it has been written off by our government. We may soon have a very rude awakening.

Transferring programs and responsibilities from the federal to local governments, reducing the size of the bureaucracy, reducing federal interference in local affairs—all these are desirable. However, whether we like it or not, any realistic discussion of the New Federalism will have to focus on the increasing disparities and imbalance facing this country. Class disparities and regional disparities carry with them a federal responsibility. No one can seriously doubt today, looking at our older cities, our older industries, our less educated and poorer population, that a huge shift in national wealth is taking place from one part of the country to another: from cities to suburbs; from poor to rich. These shifts will accelerate if federal initiatives are not taken to reverse them. As now proposed, the New Federalism would aggravate these imbalances rather than attenuate them. How can this be in the national interest, or even in the interest of the regions that are currently more prosperous?

The first debate on federalism took place in Philadelphia more than two hundred years ago. It has continued ever since. Although institutions have changed remarkably, the issues remain fundamentally the same. How can we best maintain the social justice, human dignity and equality of opportunity that are indistinguishable from the rights to life, liberty and the pursuit of happiness? The founding fathers, after more than a decade of dissatisfaction with the Articles of Confederation, concluded that these goals could not be achieved without a strong federal government. I believe that is still true today.

The federal government was created to do far more than simply carry mail or make bombs. It was chartered by the Constitution "to promote the general welfare." For the New Federalism to be meaningful, it must first of all be built on a stable national economic and social base. Most important, it must recognize and enable those states under greatest pressure to maintain adequate social services, to protect their tax bases and thereby to participate in the future growth and prosperity of the nation. This is not the case today. If the economy can be stabilized, it may be possible next year. However, if the economy is still in deep trouble a year from now, we will have many more urgent tasks than the New Federalism.

New York Review of Books, April 29, 1982

Chapter Five

———— ‿❧ ————————————————————————————

MUCH HAS BEEN WRITTEN ABOUT CONTROLLING
inflation, and much has been tried. Wage/price controls,
tax-based incomes policies and other forms of legislated
approaches have been considered. I do not believe in
wage/price controls, and I am skeptical of legislated solutions.
I tend to favor an approach to labor contracts similar to what
is practiced in Germany and Japan. I outlined this in a speech
to the League of Women Voters prior to the start of New
York's municipal labor negotiations in 1982. I favor
year-to-year contracts without cost-of-living adjustments
(COLAs) and with significant profit-sharing features.

Several months after this speech, New York City and its
labor unions settled on two-year contracts calling for
approximately 16 percent in wage increases (8 percent each
year). This occurred at a time when the rate of inflation was at
about 5 percent annually and decreasing. It was exactly such a
result to which the following remarks were addressed.

This will cost the city some $500 million *over and above* the
rate of inflation. At the very least, the second year of wage
increases should have been scaled back to the current rate of
inflation to reduce future increases in public transport fares,
personnel cuts and taxes, and to maintain the city's competitive
position. It would have been a difficult and awkward
negotiation and might not have been possible. The need for it
could have been avoided by a one-year contract. The second
year would have been negotiated at a time when it was obvious
that economic conditions had changed, the rate of inflation

significantly reduced, and quite different terms would have been the result.

At the time of this speech we were in the trough of the recession and going into an election year for the governorship of New York. Governor Hugh Carey, a lame duck, had vetoed a number of the legislature's spending measures but was unable to obtain enactment of revenue measures.

Governor Mario Cuomo, who was elected in the fall of 1982, was subsequently successful in enacting a significant tax program as well as the beginning of a state assumption of local Medicaid costs so vital to New York City. This major new source of state aid, together with revenue growth from the economic recovery, enabled the city to close its budget gap and wind up with a surplus. New York City's credit-worthiness now seems assured, as well as its present capacity to maintain budget balance.

This does not excuse a settlement that was needlessly expensive and which will make this year's labor negotiations all the more difficult. Furthermore, New York's competitive struggle to maintain its employment and tax base is far from over; on the contrary, troublesome signs abound.

These subsequent events have reinforced the views I expressed before the League of Women Voters. I believe that the principles I suggest can be applied to industrial as well as public service employees. Such a rough but practical incomes policy can be important in preventing inflation from rekindling as the recovery strengthens, while being fair to labor and to management.

Wage Policy and
New York City's Budget

FOR THE FIRST TIME SINCE 1975, THE STATE OF THE STATE and the state of the nation may be worse than the state of the city. This is due partly to economic factors and partly to political ones; the net result for the city, however, may be exceedingly grim if great care is not exercised.

From 1975 to 1980, as New York City came back from the edge of bankruptcy not only to solvency but to a high level of economic activity, we functioned in an environment that was relatively benign. The state of New York was in a consistently strong economic and fiscal position; the national economy was, by and large, buoyant, although beset by high inflation; an undervalued dollar together with political stresses in Europe and the Middle East contributed to an influx of both foreign money and its wealthy owners. In one way or another, all of these factors contributed mightily to our recovery.

More important, a few more years of similar trends are needed to bring New York City to a totally safe harbor. We in the city need a state of New York with the ability and the political will to commence a phased takeover of our Medicaid costs; we need a strong national economy to maintain our revenue growth and keep our poverty and unemployment-related costs under control; we need low interest rates and healthy credit markets to permit the city to finance itself independently. We may be cruelly disappointed on all of these counts.

The city's current situation is difficult, though not, as yet, critical; we can make it critical if we do not exercise the greatest restraint. A budgetary deficit of $750 million for fiscal 1983 is the current forecast; it is a large gap, but it can be closed through a combination of stringent cost control, continuation of the current relatively strong levels of revenue collection, modest tax increases and reasonable levels of state and federal aid. We must abort, before it gets out of control, a trend of expenditure growth that is currently outpacing expected revenue growth.

At the same time, we must be mindful of the fact that, in our competitive position with other parts of the country, our high taxes and deteriorating services are beginning to push taxpayers out again after a hiatus of several years. In the shadow of a few highly publicized moves to the Sunbelt, such as that of Harcourt Brace, a quiet exodus is taking place of less spectacular but very important operations: American Express credit cards to Salt Lake City; Citibank credit cards to South Dakota; countless back-office operations from Manhattan to various parts of the country, but not to Brooklyn, Staten Island or Queens. Slowly but surely we are starting to bleed again.

While this is happening, both the state and the nation are entering dangerous times. The New York state legislature, faced with an election year and a lame-duck governor, passed a budget that is badly out of balance. Ignoring requests for new revenues in the form of gasoline and sales taxes to pay for the requirements of transportation, education and Medicaid, New York state is left with no new revenues, no Medicaid takeover and a large looming deficit. Governor Carey's vetoes will create uncertainty about the eventual outcome, but will not create new revenues. The suggestion has been made that after the election this fall, the legislature may come back and deal with the difficult problems. That is not good enough. *Same Time, Next Year* was very good theater; it is no way to run a government.

For the city, two critical issues are involved. First, the absence of a Medicaid takeover (a billion-dollar item in our budget) is literally a matter of life and death. Second, any shadow cast over the state's credit becomes a large cloud over the city's credit. State deficits are bad for the state; they are worse for the city.

Things get worse as we work our way up to the national level. The present deep recession, high unemployment, continuing high real interest rates and strong deflationary forces have created a situation in which financial structures are exceedingly fragile and social tensions will build up again. Federal budgetary deficits at hitherto unimagined peacetime levels require that the President lead the Congress to perform major surgery. Again, the bitter fruit of an election year is paralysis; whatever action is finally taken may be too little or too late. The result could be continued high interest rates with either an aborted recovery as the optimistic scenario or an accelerating degradation of the economy as the pessimistic one.

In Washington we have witnessed the same play as in Albany. All this has serious implications for New York City:

- We have no reliable data at this point as to the expected levels of federal and state aid.
- Over the last few years, a major factor in our budget balancing was the collection of over $1 billion of unanticipated revenue resulting from high levels of inflation, but the recession has brought inflation down dramatically. Business is declining, and, sooner or later, revenues will follow suit.
- MAC will go out of business two years from now, and the city's ability to raise $1 billion annually for capital infrastructure in the public markets will depend on its ability to balance its budget *as well as* to maintain a healthy economy, with reasonable levels of services and taxes. The mayor's priority to balance the budget first and then to address himself to service improvements and capital reconstruction was absolutely correct. However, if current trends continue, the perception that budget balance is achieved only as a result of service reductions and tax increases will become more acute. The city's fragile and hard-won credit will be put in question.
- As President Reagan discovered, and as New York's Mayor Abe Beame discovered before him, the financial markets are the ultimate skeptics. The markets require budget realities and not expectations. Their reactions to President Reagan's program were not dissimilar to their skepticism of Mayor Beame's budgetary resolve. Playing "catch-up" with the markets is very difficult; cosmetic measures will not do.

New York City cannot permit itself to follow the examples of Washington and Albany; we cannot carry on with "business as usual" and wait for a crisis to compel us to shift gears. We cannot, for instance, follow Albany's example and enter into labor contracts that are clearly beyond our ability to finance. No responsible person can predict a crisis with certainty; however, any responsible observer looking at the city, state, national and international situations must conclude that the levels of risk have increased dramatically. In New York City we are at the bottom of the pyramid and we must protect ourselves.

In terms of our city economy, we must establish the principle that if taxes are increased (as some undoubtedly should be), then services must be improved.

We can have no illusions about dramatic productivity or management improvements. They come slowly when they come at all. The introduction of the two-man sanitation truck, replacing the three-man truck, was a real achievement, but one that took years to effect; it is the exception rather than the rule.

Nor can we expect significant reductions in the city's work force. We have already sustained major cutbacks. Further reductions could occur only when the city decides to eliminate or reduce entire city functions. This has clearly been impossible thus far. If anything, employment may have to be increased somewhat in such areas as police and fire protection.

I have always been a proponent of a relentless drive to reduce municipal employment through steady, managed attrition and productivity, but we cannot expect significant near-term savings from that approach. My reluctant but inescapable conclusion is that budget realities require our employment costs to remain stable since our employment levels may have to do so, and since we no longer have the luxury of our past growth in revenues.

The automotive industry and the United Auto Workers waited until one of their major companies effectively went bankrupt, the rest of the industry had become a disaster and 300,000 workers were laid off before creating a new labor-management relationship. Job security was exchanged for wage and cost-of-living freezes; profit-sharing and labor-management productivity concepts were introduced. The viability of the industry was recognized as paramount. These principles must be adopted regarding the city's relationship with its unions. The practice of confrontation must be replaced with an imperative for cooperation.

Many of these principles were actually adopted during the early stages of the city crisis in 1975–1976, after the large initial wage cuts and layoffs. They were subsequently relaxed and later abandoned in the boom of the late 1970s. We have no choice but to go back and start over again, because circumstances compel us to do so. I recognize that calling for such a change at a time when arbitrators are weighing the MTA contract is awkward timing, but the fact that arbitration was required for that contract underlines the need for a new relationship.

Municipal labor negotiations are about to start in the city. There is never a good time for wrenching changes; at the same time, the state of the national economy and the reduction in the inflation rate requires us to act.

At a time of great uncertainty, of sharp fluctuations in prices, interest rates and unemployment levels, the only thing we can be certain of is our inability to predict economic performance with accuracy. In both Germany and Japan, labor negotiations take place within the framework of year-to-year agreements, based on economic assumptions agreed upon by business, labor and government, and retrospective adjustments at the end of the period. The automatic wage increases and cost-of-living adjustments (COLAs) contained in multi-year contracts are thus eliminated and the concept of participation in actual performance is substituted. This concept, together with those of current automobile contracts, should be tried here.

The near-term outlook for the economy is so weak and the rate of inflation so low that what might have appeared six months ago to be a reasonably austere contract by historical standards may turn out to be far beyond the city's ability to pay. The state of the economy and the continuing drop in the inflation rate call for levels of restraint we have not witnessed since 1975–1976. If the traditional process of signing multi-year contracts is to be maintained, it must be based on levels of increases below the current rate of inflation. The risks of doing otherwise, both to the city and to its labor force, are too great to permit anything else. If long-term commitments have to be made, we have to err on the side of caution. The result of doing otherwise as reality comes forward could be large layoffs, further service reductions, a renewed exodus of taxpayers and the beginning of a new downward budgetary spiral that would be harmful to both the city and its labor force.

One must recognize, however, that abrupt changes in the economic climate are possible. It is also not irrational to imagine in the longer term that the federal government's inability to revive the economy in the next year or so, coupled with a number of large bankruptcies or credit crunches, could bring on attempts at rapid reflation. This could lead to a resumption of inflation at much higher rates, beyond anything now foreseeable. Two or three years down the road, today's multi-year contract could be harmful to the workers and to the city for a number of different reasons.

If the present collective bargaining process does not produce stability with reasonable protection to both the city and its work force, a different statewide process may have to be considered. If the city is to be maintained as a competitive entity vis-à-vis the Sunbelt localities, and if taxes have to be raised and employment levels maintained to provide adequate services, one-year contracts could be negotiated by the city and its unions in lieu of the traditional multi-year ones. The prospective wage increase would be set below the rate of inflation. Since the inflation rate could well come down to a low single-digit number, the city's revenue growth could be significantly reduced. However, this would also mean that no intolerable burden would be placed on the workers as a result of actual cost-of-living increases. During the first year of the process, which would have to be statewide, a commission including representatives of the state, the city, the labor leadership and the private sector should draw up guidelines for the new process of creating labor contracts. These would include:

- the institutionalization of year-to-year contracts, with no COLAs, without eliminating collective bargaining
- a process for setting retrospective adjustments or bonuses, based on actual economic performance (this would include the concept of profit-sharing whereby employees may be rewarded with larger than expected compensation, and the taxpayers with tax reduction or service improvements if the economy performs better than expected)
- a review of possibly different concepts of long-term job security as part of such a process

I realize this is a lot easier said than done; many variations on this theme could accomplish the same objectives—for example, multi-year contracts with annual adjustment clauses. But there has to be a will for change. The answer to those who will say it cannot be done would be to suggest that both the auto industry and the UAW probably wish they had not waited all these years to face reality. Had they acted five years ago, tens of thousands of jobs might have been saved and Japanese cars would not account for 20 percent of U.S. sales. Houston, Dallas and Phoenix are to New York City what Toyota and Honda are to the Ford Motor Company.

This new approach, coupled with other proposed tax and local actions, would go a long way toward closing our current budget gap credibly. Federal and state budget actions taken later this year or next, the actual performance of our economy, our actual and anticipated rates of inflation would all be taken into account in setting retrospective adjustments and would become the basis for the following year's labor negotiations. The time to start is now.

It is easy to forget that access to the capital markets for the city is but a recent phenomenon. The city still does not have the investment-grade credit ratings on its bonds that will be needed to be self-sufficient for its long-term capital needs. Confidence in the city's ability to control its costs, in a period of slow revenue growth, is required if the city is to have any chance at financial self-sufficiency. By 1984 the city will have to raise $1 billion annually, as MAC goes out of existence in December 1984, as provided by law, having by then functioned for ten years and raised $10 billion.

The belief exists, as always, that there is an easy solution to the city's financing problem. This supposedly easy solution would be to extend MAC's life and increase its borrowing authority by legislative action beyond 1984. The fact that this would be fiscally irresponsible does not guarantee that it will not happen. It is good, however, to remind those who harbor this belief not to repeat the illusions of 1975. Then there was the notion that the mere existence of MAC meant the availability of large amounts of essentially unconditional credit to the city. There is no such thing as unconditional credit. Credit is both fragile and fickle; it should not be taken for granted.

I have been in business for over thirty years, and I do not recall a time before today that challenged so many notions, created so many risks and at the same time provided such opportunities to start afresh. For the city and its labor leadership, the opportunity is there to form a new partnership. Once before, we let this opportunity slip from our grasp as the crisis of 1975 receded from our memories. If we let it slip this time, the next crisis may not be quite so forgiving.

Speech to the League of Women Voters,
New York City, April 20, 1982

Chapter Six

———— ೭☙ ————————————————

IN THE SUMMER OF 1981 I WROTE A CRITIQUE OF
Reaganomics for *The Economist.* The enthusiasm for
supply-side economics, together with the new President's
budget and tax victories in the Congress, had created political
euphoria. The Conservative Revolution had arrived. Looking
back, I note that inflation and interest rates came down more
rapidly than I had anticipated, as did oil prices; on the other
hand, the recession was much more severe. Real interest rates
are still high today, but the Federal Reserve has considerably
loosened its monetary policy since 1981. The recovery, at the
time of this writing, is more vigorous than was generally
expected.

I still believe the Administration needlessly gambled our
economic future by creating huge and continuing deficits and
relying on unproven theories to close them. This is our
Achilles heel, and it still remains to be dealt with.

I believe that economic recovery will bring the issue of
fairness to the fore more starkly than in times of recession.
Sharp increases in corporate profits will be weighed against a
small decrease in unemployment. Skills and education will be
elusive for large numbers looking for work. Regional
differences will be aggravated.

The current performance of the economy reaffirms my
conviction that an equitable relationship among freedom,
fairness and wealth remains terribly elusive. A conservative
government has largely ignored the question of fairness in
shaping its economic policies. Sooner or later, a more moderate

and equitable approach will have to replace current policies.

I find our energy situation still one of our most baffling and frustrating problems. The weakness of OPEC provides us with an opportunity to redress some of the injuries of the 1970s. This means further encouraging oil price reductions with an oil-import fee, as well as increasing gasoline taxes. It means continuing the search for domestic oil and gas as well as the development of alternate sources of energy such as coal and synthetic fuels. But other than the tiny five-cent-per-gallon gas tax voted last winter, no significant moves for energy taxes have succeeded. Neither conservatives nor liberals seem willing to grasp this nettle.

Since I wrote this essay, probably the most significant practical developments have been major changes in the Reagan Administration's program and a strong economic recovery. The first change was the abandonment of strict monetarism by the Federal Reserve Board in the summer of 1982 in favor of an expansionary monetary policy. The second was the $99 billion tax package of 1982 together with the explicit recognition of the need for more revenues in the proposal for "standby taxes" in the 1983 budget. The rhetoric of the Administration may still be "supply-side," but the actions are Keynesian: deficits to spur recovery, expectations of consumer spending, expectation of increased tax revenues as the economy expands.

Inflation has been significantly reduced, partly as a result of wage settlements much more austere than I anticipated, as well as reduced food and fuel costs. Interest rates have come down, and the economic recovery was strengthened as a result of these factors.

As I have indicated previously, I have changed my views as to the practicality of a tax-based incomes policy. However, I still believe in its objective.

There has not been, so far, a philosophically coherent answer from the opposition. Liberals have brought up the issues of fairness and peace and a nuclear freeze. But they have yet to develop a position of "tough moderation" that will explain how to encourage growth and fairness within the framework of a balanced budget and that will deal with the peace issue within the framework of the reality of Soviet power.

America
in the 1980s

BUSINESS/LABOR/GOVERNMENT COOPERATION COUPLED
with courageous, interventionist political leadership saved New
York City. Wealth, freedom and fairness were the subjects of
continued, delicate tradeoffs. A wage freeze and a Financial Control
Board impinged on freedoms. Taxes, reductions in services,
job losses, increased tuition fees and public-transport fares—all
involved tradeoffs between wealth and fairness. There were no
riots and only one short strike. We succeeded by a thin margin.
We proved that intervention, liberalism and a balanced budget
were not mutually exclusive. I believe this can apply to the nation
at a time when the current theology is just the opposite.

For the democracies of the West, the last twenty years of this
century will witness continuous tradeoffs and strains among freedom,
fairness and wealth. In the United States conservatives have
consistently focused on freedom and wealth, liberals on freedom
and fairness. We have yet to build a political bridge, however, that
gives all three factors their due weight; unless we are able to do
so, we will face greater and greater difficulties.

Freedom is not an absolute; it must be tempered by justice. In
a world of finite resources, this requires political leadership of a
high order, more interested in leading than in lasting. Only rarely
will correct long-term decisions turn out to be popular.

Fairness and wealth have to go hand in hand. The "zero-sum
society" can be neither free nor fair. Without the capacity to create
wealth, it is impossible to deal with the issue of fairness. The
disparities in our society, between classes and races, between Sunbelt
and Frostbelt, are deep and getting deeper. Only with sustained
economic growth, a strong free market and an active government
willing to intervene, when needed, will these disparities
be reduced.

Fairness is also not an absolute. But the most hardened conservatives must find conditions in the inner-city ghettos a blight on our society and an indictment of the status quo. At the same time, realistic liberals have to recognize that government has not solved, and cannot solve, all the problems of race and poverty. Only a growing private-sector economy can do that, provided government is not afraid of directing some of that growth. This is obviously not what is happening today.

A conservative laissez-faire philosophy was the predictable reaction to the failed performance of liberalism at home and the eroding power and prestige of the United States abroad. The discrediting of liberalism, at least partly deserved, is a danger to our society. Yet liberalism will not become a needed counterweight to current trends until it comes back to the real world, the bread-and-butter world of jobs and growth, of urban blight and energy dependence, of the realistic need for American power in a chaotic world, and until it returns to the notion that democracy requires equality of opportunity, not an egalitarianism resolutely blind to the question of merit.

Gay rights and national health insurance may be important to some, but they are not the country's first priorities. It is liberalism's fascination with secondary issues that has created the reaction that has seen the Moral Majority intimidating politicians and advertisers, and Congress trying to determine the beginning of life. The first priority of liberalism has to be creation of wealth together with its fair allocation.

The economic aims of the Reagan Administration are impeccable: reduce government spending, reduce taxes, reduce interest rates, strengthen our defense, balance the budget. Although I fervently hope for its success, I am concerned by the inherent contradictions of these aims. The result may well be continued inflation and slow growth, combined with greater and greater disparities as oil, defense contracts and sunshine favor half the United States while the other half drifts more and more off into the shadows. No democracy, not even one as large as ours, can survive half suburb and half slum. The equation between wealth and fairness will become more and more elusive. The result may ultimately be the loss of freedom.

A number of factors currently threaten the economic and social stability of the Western world. Energy dependence, inflation, chronic unemployment and slow growth are all interrelated, and a drain on the West. However, probably no single economic issue in the Western world is more critical today than the level of interest rates. Far from being a simple reflection of economic policies and underlying inflation rates, interest rates and money supply have been made by the cult of monetarism into a cure for inflation they can never hope to be.*

In theory, supply-side economics looks for politically painless answers to agonizingly complicated questions. It argues that revenue growth from the stimulus of tax cuts will accommodate defense increases and balance the budget; that reductions in spending will come out of waste and fraud. At the same time, monetarists argue that controlling the supply of money, regardless of interest rates, is supposed to reduce inflation, no matter what the current budget deficits. Compounding these apparently contradictory policies is an argument by supply-siders for a prompt return to the gold standard to take the pressure off the financial markets.

Some rationality was introduced into this process when the Administration decided that a totally painless scenario was impossible and that an attempt had to be made to lower government spending by steep and lasting budget cuts. The hoped-for scenario now seems to call for the economy to be induced into a short, sharp recession by tight money, with lower inflation resulting from budget cuts and slow monetary growth, and with the stimulus of tax cuts coupled with an increased savings rate providing, by mid-1982, the basis for strong, noninflationary, budget-balancing growth.† At the same time, Wall Street is sharply criticized for its skepticism, as reflected by continued high interest rates; ardent

---

*Monetarism did produce a sharp reduction in inflation. It did so while producing the steepest recession since World War II and creating 35 million unemployed in the Western world. It was, as a practical matter, abandoned in the summer of 1982 when the Federal Reserve reversed itself dramatically in order to prevent the defaults of Mexico and Brazil, as well as to avoid a banking crisis. As of this writing, pure monetarism appears to be a dead issue.

†Part of this scenario happened. The economy went into a steep recession and inflation was sharply cut. However, the turnaround (which came in 1983) occurred as a result of significantly more stimulative monetary policy and consumer spending while budget deficits are greater than ever. Real interest rates are still prohibitively high and government borrowing is a threat to the recovery.

supporters of the free market take to task the freest market of all, the bond market, for disagreeing with their analysis.

President Reagan is a man clearly endowed with firm philosophical convictions and great personal qualities. He has so far brilliantly dominated the political agenda and changed the direction of social and economic America more fundamentally than anyone since President Roosevelt in 1932 with the passage of his budget and three-year tax cuts.

But the money markets are the ultimate realists, and they respond according to the following assumptions:

- that America may be running huge budgetary deficits for several years to come
- that several sectors of the American economy, most importantly those related to energy and defense, are comparatively impervious to interest rates and will compete with the government and the balance of the private sector for huge amounts of capital
- that interest rates do not slow down inflation even if they slow down the economy, since wage and price behavior in many areas seems unrelated to economic activity; high interest rates are more likely to add to inflation than to reduce it
- that the impact of proposed increases in military expenditures will require massive amounts of credit and scarce skilled labor, creating their own inflationary push

The impact on both sides of the Atlantic of interest rates at or near their current levels can be devastating. Even assuming a mild decline from current levels, the European economies will be in dire straits and one half of the United States will be in serious difficulties.

The need for a fallback alternative to current policies seems clear. What courses of action are open if, twelve months from now, America still has high interest rates, slow economic growth and a series of industries (savings and loan associations, housing, airlines, steel, cars) as well as a number of cities in real trouble? There is no safety net in place to deal selectively with industrial or regional problems which could come soon and in considerable size. If, twelve months from now, the Administration's program has not sufficiently stimulated investment and reduced inflation, the only course left at that time might be wage, price and credit controls coupled with savage further reductions in budgetary expenditure.

This would occur in a social climate strained not only by economic and social hardship for the older half of the United States, but by a series of highly divisive social issues brought to the fore by extreme conservatives. The coming year will see abortion, busing, voting rights, school prayer and the death penalty passionately argued in Congress. The debate over these issues will not create an atmosphere conducive to resolving an economic crisis that might occur at the same time.

It would have been both fairer and safer to aim at budget balance initially, thus lowering the credit requirements of the government, creating lower interest rates as a result of the lesser borrowings of government, and only then triggering the major portion of the tax cuts. Fairness and common sense require that the tax cuts be more restrained in the aggregate and more evenly distributed among income groups. Fairness requires that additional budget cuts include programs benefiting the middle class (Social Security, cost-of-living allowances, federal pensions, Medicare) as well as those benefiting the poor (federally funded training programs for the unemployed, Medicaid, welfare). Also, the present notion that a three-year tax cut guarantees future budget cuts is erroneous. Left to its own devices, Congress will run deficits. Future tax cuts should be conditional upon an equivalent amount of budget cuts in those entitlement programs that are indexed to the consumer price index but are politically difficult to interfere with.

Budget balance in the near future requires a different mix of fiscal, energy and defense policies. To begin with, it requires taxing gasoline at higher rates. The temporary glut in oil has created the illusion that our energy problem is over. Instead of being lulled by this illusion, we should take advantage of the temporary weakness of OPEC by imposing a fee on imported crude oil and/or a fifty-cent-per-gallon tax at the pump. The result would be gasoline at two dollars per gallon, still 50 percent below the European level, further downward pressure on OPEC prices and $50 billion in annual revenues for budget balance. A rebate of the tax to those in lower-income groups could be part of such a program.

America would then be in a much stronger financial position to consider massive increases in defense spending. The defense budget should be scrutinized carefully for waste. If, in the last analysis, significant increases above the present levels turn out to be justified, they should be conditioned on passage of a gasoline tax, or equivalent import fee, to pay for part of the increase.

A commitment to a strong defense requires more than money. Fairness requires the middle class to participate in the defense of our country not only with their money but with their children. A return to the draft is necessary in equity as well as economics: in equity because at present the poor and the minorities make up the majority of the volunteer army; in economics because the standards of performance of the volunteer army do not match the requirements created by the sophisticated weaponry contemplated. Enormous waste is the likely result of the present make-up of our armed services.

The creation of wealth and its fair distribution require that a bridge be built between our disadvantaged, underskilled population and the job opportunities of the future. This bridge does not exist today. It is a fantasy to suggest, as the McGill presidential commission did, that millions will travel from Detroit and Cleveland, laid-off steel workers and inner-city ghetto residents, to make semiconductors in Phoenix and drill for oil in Texas. Too many educational, cultural and racial problems will stand in the way. If urban life in the northern half of the United States continues to decay, those leaving our older cities will be those who can afford it, leaving behind a larger and larger proportion of increasingly desperate people, needing more assistance and getting less.

In the struggle to avoid the bankruptcy of New York City, the Municipal Assistance Corporation was able to play a pivotal role in the bargains that had to be struck between competing constituencies; it was the linchpin between business, labor and government regarding those prickly issues of fairness and wealth. On a national scale, a similar role could be played by a modern version of the Reconstruction Finance Corporation (RFC) which would provide capital to northern cities falling into ruin and older industries unable to face foreign competition.

The free market is inadequate to the task. Far from simply bailing out failing companies or politicians unwilling to face reality, the RFC would offer its capital only to those entities willing to make the sacrifices required to make them viable: corporations whose unions are willing to make wage and productivity concessions and rely more on profit-sharing; managements that will make equivalent sacrifices and limit price increases; stockholders who will forgo dividends in order to maximize investments. The list should include cities in states where legislatures are willing to require the suburbs to pay for their fair share of city services; where budget oversight is in structures like the New York City Financial Control Board; where public-sector unions restrain wage and pension demands; and where the business community continues to invest and build. We might finance the RFC by borrowing back on a long-term basis part of the dollar surpluses of some of the OPEC members. To encourage low interest rates we might consider a partial gold clause on those bonds, thus testing the practicality of a limited form of gold standard.*

In general, in the inner city, jobs will have to be brought to the people, since one cannot take the people to the jobs. The RFC should finance inner-city manufacturing and service facilities, operated by private business. Clearly, such employment will have to be subsidized, but its cost will be little compared with the current economic and social costs of generations on welfare, on drugs and involved in crime.

Inner-city school systems should be tied as directly as possible to employment opportunities, with the ultimate aim of being able to hold out the promise of a job if a child stays in school, off the streets and out of trouble. The "workfare" requirement being discussed by the present Administration as a prerequisite for welfare payments should be replaced by a "schoolfare" requirement; if job opportunities are created for inner-city youths graduating from school, a requirement for school attendance as part of the welfare program would be more meaningful than a requirement for menial and useless work.

The Siamese twins of crime and drugs in the cities can be opposed only by education and jobs in the ghettos. Neither the operation of the free market nor calls for the northern poor to migrate to the Sunbelt will solve that problem. The intervention of an RFC might.

---

*The notion of OPEC financing is clearly unrealistic in light of OPEC's dwindling surpluses, the result of falling oil prices and their large development commitments.

In a year or so, the more suicidal aspects of the recent tax rebellion will require sober examination. California already faces the reality of Proposition 13 with significant budgetary reductions in Los Angeles, San Francisco and other localities; Massachusetts will pay for Proposition 2½ with large cuts in Boston's police, fire and education departments. The euphoria of federal budget reductions will be replaced by the realization that a large part of the cutbacks will simply be reflected by higher local taxes for a lesser level of local services. Higher fares and poorer service on decaying public transport systems in Chicago, New York and Birmingham will bring home to people the truth that the elimination of federal transport subsidies is more than an intellectual exercise to curb inflation.

The RFC should provide low-interest loans to rebuild those systems, but on condition that the local unions contribute their share in higher productivity and that local legislatures provide adequate tax support. Public transport should be a cheap, clean, civilized substitute for the automobile; that is a matter of national self-interest. In addition, a much larger coal-based energy program, together with transport and facilities for export, would help the northern half of the country and could be financed, in part, by the RFC.

In setting an American economic and social agenda for the 1980s, the issues of regional disparities, older industries, inner-city blight and alternative energy sources must come high on the list. The RFC would have a role in each of these areas.

The current experiment in supply-side economics is a gamble, in more ways than one. In terms of pure economics, it is a gamble in that its potential for success rests on the requirement of unprecedented behavior on the part of 220 million Americans in their spending and saving patterns. It is a greater gamble in its underlying philosophy of a government with a minimal role in our social structure and an activist role almost solely limited to defense. The damage caused by excessive government regulation and interference in the 1970s will not be cured by government abdication in the 1980s.

Billions for defense do not address the issue of how an inadequately educated army will use more and more sophisticated weapons systems; no amount of accelerated depreciation will bring education and employment to the ghetto; productivity will not be improved when the sons of factory foremen increasingly want to grow up to be lawyers and management consultants instead of engineers and chemists; tax cuts will not improve the prospects for gun control in an increasingly violent society; a return to the gold standard is no substitute for fiscal responsibility on the part of political leaders.

A balanced budget is not inconsistent with liberal aspirations; in many ways, those aspirations should require it, since only thus can we have lower interest rates, lower inflation and high economic activity. An RFC, higher gasoline taxes, rebuilding older cities and older industries—these are not inconsistent with conservative aims. They are consistent with helping the supply side of the economy, financing defense and alternative energy, and creating noninflationary growth. To this agenda we should add a tax-based incomes policy, to be adopted in conjunction with such a program and which requires compromise on the part of both conservatives and liberals. Both labor and business would have to sacrifice; freedom would be abridged. However, both fairness and wealth would ultimately benefit.

Although the United States has recently been lucky in the matter of food and fuel prices, inflation will not come down sufficiently as long as wage and price behavior continues to operate independently of market forces. The tax system should be used to reward restrained wage and price behavior and to penalize excessive wage settlements or price increases, creating a rational incomes policy. As a transition measure, a temporary wage and price freeze should be enacted pending the elaboration of future policy. Wage and price controls are cumbersome and ultimately ineffectual; an incomes policy, on the other hand, could result in restrained wage and price behavior over an extended period of time.

Balanced-budget liberalism should be the liberal economic agenda for the 1980s. It should aim at the creation of wealth and its fair distribution at every level of our society and in every part of our country as well as at a realistic view of America's security needs.

Such an agenda is also more in tune with America's relationship with its Western allies as well as with the Third World. America's interdependence with the rest of the Western world requires economic policies that are not diametrically opposed to those of its allies. At the same time, the West as a whole, as a matter of enlightened self-interest, must try as much as possible to promote the economic survival of the Third World. Although OPEC must supply much of the financing for the Third World, lower interest rates and higher rates of growth in the West are essential for its survival.

A predominantly free economy is a necessity; a totally free market is a myth. Conservatives will find that they cannot be partially virginal as far as the free market is concerned. As long as so-called voluntary car export restraints are demanded of the Japanese, we should go further and require wage restraints from the United Auto Workers and price restraint from auto industry managements. Conservatives will have to recognize that providing a $6 billion tax windfall to savings and loan associations neither is consistent with their philosophy nor will solve the problem. Liberals, on the other hand, will have to learn to treat government spending as if it were their own money, because it is.

Americans do not live in a free-market economy today. The prices of energy, food and credit are not freely set. Americans live in a mixed economy, predominantly free-market-oriented, but in which the government plays and must continue to play an important role. It must be an active participant, along with business and labor, in striking those bargains which are required to apportion benefits and sacrifice as evenly as possible among various constituencies.

In less than twenty years we have gone from the American Century to the American Crisis. This is partly a result of the postwar growth in the economic power of Western Europe, Japan and Southeast Asia as well as the projection of the military and geopolitical power of Russia. At first we lived with the illusion that our own postwar economic and military superiority meant that our resources knew no limits. Then there were many self-inflicted wounds: Vietnam; Watergate; business and union leaders showing as little fiscal restraint as our political leaders; the snapshot quality of television news and the demise of the written press; our failure to react to the oil embargo with harsh financial and physical conservation measures; runaway budget deficits eroding our currency and our economy.

However, the United States has enormous opportunities. Becoming more self-sufficient in energy, rebuilding our basic industries and our older cities—there is work here for everyone in this country as far as the eye can see. Of course, we need tax cuts, lower inflation and interest rates, regulatory reform and a balanced budget. An activist President working in partnership with business and labor will be needed to make that happen.

The voters of Western democracies seem more and more willing to experiment ideologically in order to find satisfactory economic performance. The danger in such experimentation is their possible willingness to turn to extremes if they believe all else has failed. If the current economic program fails, with its underlying conservative and nearly radical social philosophy, there will be only two choices. Either a middle-of-the-road philosophy, halfway between the deficit-spending liberalism of the 1960s and the current conservatism, will evolve and prevail, or we may go to extremes.

As a nation, we clearly have the resources—financial, technical and intellectual—to solve our problems. Whether we have the political will and the commitment is another question. Questions of fairness and wealth must be answered by today's politicians. The answers will determine whether, in a world of limited resources, Western democracy can make the necessary tradeoffs and simultaneously maintain freedom. Our biggest danger does not consist of a group of old men sitting in the Kremlin, worrying about Poland and Afghanistan.

The New Deal and the Great Society were the great liberal economic watersheds of this century. They were fundamentally different in their aims and results. The New Deal sought to put people to work and curb the excesses of the 1920s; it also saved the capitalistic system in America. The RFC, CCC, REA, and TVA all aimed at stimulating production and employment; they succeeded. The SEC, Social Security, the Federal Reserve Board, the FDIC and antitrust laws were aimed at regulating excesses and protecting the public; they succeeded. The Great Society, on the other hand, aimed at cradle-to-grave security, income transfer, elimination of poverty, pervasive regulation; to the extent it failed, it did so largely because America could not afford it. By attempting to reduce the risk, it succeeded in eliminating many of the incentives to create wealth.

The riots of Liverpool and Manchester carry a message similar to those of Watts and Miami. The message is despair, and it cannot be ignored. Yet while we are entitled to expect an appropriate level of involvement from our government, we cannot expect it to do everything; a just middle ground has to evolve. If we can build on what we have, if we reject the notion that there are simple answers to agonizingly complicated problems, we can solve our problems at home and have enormous ideological impact abroad. There are no permanent solutions to ever-changing problems. We do not need to plan for a hundred years, but we need a government that is pragmatic and flexible, willing to intervene when necessary.

I doubt that today's conservatism will provide all the answers. Liberalism's hour may come again. To meet the test, however, liberalism will have to come out of the political boudoir and get back to the inner-city streets, to the factory floor and to the defense of our vital interests. Because that is where reality lies.

The Economist, September 19, 1981

Chapter Seven

FOR SEVERAL YEARS I HAVE ARGUED, PUBLICLY AND privately, for the creation of a 1980s version of the Reconstruction Finance Corporation (RFC) of the 1930s. Early in 1981 Robert Silvers, editor of the *New York Review of Books,* asked me to put my thoughts in writing. Obviously, much has occurred since then and much has changed.

The reported earnings of our basic industries were somewhat better in 1982 than at the time of this essay. However, when tax credits, accounting devices and diversification were eliminated, the basic underlying operating results were still dismal. The 1983 recovery will show significant further improvement, particularly in the automobile industry, but we are still at considerable risk from foreign competition.

Chrysler has done significantly better than I expected thanks to the efforts and talent of Lee Iacocca and his management, the cooperation of the United Auto Workers and an economic recovery stronger than I expected. Lee Iacocca would be the first, however, to recognize that Chrysler is not out of the woods and would be better off with an RFC, despite its early repayment of the government-guaranteed loans. Also, if Chrysler is ultimately successful, an RFC might have provided an opportunity for the taxpayers to have a greater share in the benefits as well as the risks.

The possibility of OPEC providing part of the financing for the RFC out of its surpluses is no longer realistic in the light of falling oil prices, even though the United States is still paying out about $50 billion annually for imported oil.

However, there are many alternative financial possibilities. I have tried to indicate the RFC does not consist of either "picking winners" or "bailing out losers," but is rather an instrument for negotiation and restructuring. I have used the name RFC rather than some other because it stands for what I believe in, i.e., the need for reconstruction and capital. Its ancestor in the 1930s performed, with great success, some of the functions that a new RFC would perform. But the 1980s are different from the 1930s and the new RFC would be as different from the old one as a Boeing 747 is from a Ford Tri-Motor.

I still believe that regional shifts and the likelihood of increasing regional differences are some of this country's most serious and least recognized problems. It is politically difficult to do so, but sooner or later these problems will be addressed.

Implicit in any effort to achieve regional balance and stimulate industrial and infrastructure investment is the necessity that we do something to improve life in the inner-city ghetto. Regional development corporations as well as city and state business/labor groups should be created with the RFC. If the auto industry and midwestern cities are to get new funds, the program should include inner-city manufacturing facilities tied directly to inner-city school systems, union commitments to minority apprenticeship and possibly two-tier minimum wages during training. These programs should be run by private industry, in facilities financed by an RFC and leased to the companies, in the same manner as were the defense plants during World War II.

Mao Tse-tung believed that power for political change grew out of the barrel of a gun. I believe that power for political change can grow out of the actions of economic institutions. Jean Monnet changed the political face of Europe by creating the European Coal and Steel Authority. An RFC could create the environment that would permit the execution of industrial policy, regional policy and possibly incomes policy, which are needed but have no present constituency in the United States.

There are, of course, dangers in creating an RFC. The potential for political influence, corruption or inefficiency is always present. Much will depend on the professionalism of the people who run it, on a charter that provides the proper combination of public accountability and shelter from political pressures, and on the public's perception that the RFC is performing in the public interest. These were the main ingredients for the success of the Municipal Assistance Corporation.

I believe there is an overall concept worth exploring here: namely, that the United States should be looked upon as a continent and not merely a country, and that half of this continent is turning into an underdeveloped country in need of development assistance.

The reader will find that in my more recent essays and testimony I have limited somewhat the scope and size of the RFC. Instead of functioning as an independent entity, it would be the financing agency of a tripartite board appointed by the President. I believe such an approach is more in tune with political realities and is also sounder. There will always be opportunity to increase its scope once it has a proven record of achievement.

Although the economic environment has changed since 1981, I believe that the need for an RFC grows every day. Because of the present recovery, the political climate for it is still not propitious, but I suspect that some version of such an institution will be in existence within five years.

Reconstructing America

ONE OF THE GRAVEST EVENTS IN OUR HISTORY IS THE migration taking place within the United States. During the last decade Chicago lost 12 percent of its population, Baltimore 14 percent, Cleveland 24 percent and St. Louis 28 percent. The proportion of taxpayers moving out was undoubtedly greater. During this period Houston gained 24 percent, San Diego 25 percent, Phoenix 33 percent. A recent study by the Industrial Conference Board measured regional standards of living by examining cost of living and household income in eighteen metropolitan areas. By those measurements, residents of northeastern metropolitan areas had living standards 25 to 33 percent below those of their southern and western counterparts.

During the same period, some of the most important American industries have been failing badly. In 1979 U.S. Steel lost almost one-half billion dollars. In 1980 the Ford Motor Company, Chrysler and General Motors each lost between $1.5 and $2 billion, International Harvester almost $500 million and Firestone $100 million.

It is no coincidence that the cities under the greatest strain are tied to the industries in the most severe difficulty, particularly in the region extending from Baltimore to St. Louis. Existing trends are likely to exacerbate rather than attenuate this situation, with the result that another decade like the last one will divide the country into "have" and "have-not" regions with unpredictable but probably highly unpleasant consequences. As taxpayers leave older urban centers, the remaining tax base collapses inward, requiring higher taxes for a population that is unable to pay them and fewer services for people in increasing need of them. In these trends are the makings of social strife.

At the same time, our traditionally powerful industries, the industrial locomotives that drove this country for the last century, are in the throes of a similar self-eviscerating cycle. Harshly affected by foreign competition, unable to raise vast amounts of capital needed to modernize, they live from hand to mouth, not investing in the future in order to survive today. They are also affected by a deep structural shift not only in regional prosperity but, as Emma Rothschild recently wrote, in the basic nature of American work as well—the shift away from productive industry toward consumer and retail services, notably "eating and drinking places" (including fast-food restaurants) and health and business services. As Ms. Rothschild wrote, these three industries together

accounted for more than 40 percent of the new private jobs created between 1973 and the summer of 1980. In that period their employment increased almost three times as fast as total private employment, and sixteen times as fast as employment in the goods-producing or industrial sector of the economy.

. . . The *increase* in employment in eating and drinking places since 1973 is greater than total employment in the automobile and steel industries combined. Total employment in the three industries is greater than total employment in an entire range of basic productive industries: construction, all machinery, all electric and electronic equipment, motor vehicles, aircraft, ship building, all chemicals and products, and all scientific and other instruments.*

Allocating blame for these trends is easy—there is enough for everyone. Government regulation has been costly and ill-advised, and so have government policies, particularly with respect to energy, including the cowardly avoidance of taxing gasoline at much higher rates. Weak managements and short-sighted unions have collaborated in the creation of inefficient organizations whose costs are high and productivity low. Research and development, on which industrial productivity heavily depends, have been inadequate in the United States in both quality and quantity. We have produced an educational system that ignores the crafts and a culture that idolizes rock stars.

The fact that practically everyone is to blame does not mean,

*"Reagan and the Real America," *New York Review of Books,* February 5, 1981.

however, that we should throw up our hands. It means rather that we must accept shared sacrifices to reverse the trend. The United States today, in its basic productive industries, needs a second Industrial Revolution. The currently fashionable notion of backing the winners instead of the losers is as facile as it is shallow. The losers today are the automotive, steel, glass, rubber and other basic industries. That this nation can continue to function while writing off such industries to foreign competition strikes me as nonsense. Nor does it seem to me workable in the long run for a larger and larger proportion of our population to be diverted to such jobs as serving food and processing business paper while the industries that manufacture products for sale at home and abroad decline.

We cannot become a nation of short-order cooks and saleswomen, Xerox operators and messenger boys. These jobs are a weak basis for the economy; with their short hours and low pay, they are easily eliminated in prolonged downturns. To let other countries make things while we concentrate on services is debilitating both in its substance and in its symbolism. The argument that we are substituting brains for brawn is specious; brains without sinews are not good enough.

When our basic industries fail, moreover, the shareholders and the workers who are laid off are not the only ones to suffer. Nothing is more inflationary than unemployment when it is coupled with trade adjustment payments, on top of benefits, on top of welfare. What we have to do is to turn the losers into winners, restructure our basic industries to make them competitive and use whatever U.S. government resources are necessary to do the job.

This country's goal must be twofold: first, to have a functioning economy with stable growth and emphasis on the creation of private-sector jobs; and second, to have all elements of our society, and all regions of the country, participate in that growth as fully as possible.

It is not only foreign competition that challenges our basic industries. We depend on highly unstable countries not just for our basic energy supply but also for the strength or weakness of the dollar. And the regional shifts in national wealth I have mentioned will, partly as a result of oil and gas price decontrol, threaten our social and economic stability as a nation if allowed to continue unchecked.

From 1980 to 1990, decontrol of oil and gas prices will generate about $120 billion of revenues to the energy-producing regions of this country. This is a tax that will be paid by the consuming regions of the Northeast and Midwest in the form of royalties and severance taxes. At the same time, a program of heavy tax cuts intended to shore up the "supply side" of the economy is bound to accelerate the movement of manufacturing businesses away from the northern part of the country. The federal budget cutbacks that will have a heavy impact in the Northeast and the Midwest will be more than made up in the Sunbelt by increases in revenues resulting from energy pricing as well as sharp increases in defense spending. With these revenues local taxes in the Sunbelt states can be reduced, services maintained and all kinds of incentives provided for industry. The drain of businesses away from the Northeast and the Midwest will obviously increase, with the inevitable deterioration of the regional tax base.

We will then be faced with a situation in which one city after another in the north of the country will be less and less able to support a larger and larger proportion of its population in need of public assistance. The industries that formerly provided employment and support will continue to decline. Many of those taxpayers who are able to leave will migrate to the Sunbelt, leaving behind a growing mass of unemployed or unemployable people unable to move or afraid to try. Not even a country as large as ours can maintain its democratic institutions half rich and half poor, especially when the economic trends will make it very apparent that for the "have nots" things will get worse and not better.

There has been much talk recently about "reindustrialization" and "industrial policy." The former ("lemon socialism" to its detractors) is described as a government bailout of the large and inefficient industries and companies. The latter is a policy by which the government would deliberately "pick the winners" and provide for their accelerated development. Except for additional tax benefits for research and development, however, attempts by government to "pick the winners" are for the most part futile. No government agency is capable of doing so, and in fact, the winners do very nicely without being selected for special government help. Such efficient users of new technology as IBM, Hewlett-Packard, Tektronix and Intel have been spectacular successes in the 1950s,

1960s and 1970s. There is no need for the government to try to identify their counterparts for the 1980s and 1990s; they will emerge by themselves.

It is also counterproductive for government to bail out large, inefficient or noncompetitive organizations if the only result is to have them limp along, neither dead nor alive, a menace to their healthier competitors and to themselves. A case in point is the so-called rescue of Chrysler, which is nevertheless doomed to failure, at a heavy cost to the taxpayer, because the remedy was inappropriate to the disease.*

What is needed is, first, an industrial policy committed to restructing basic U.S. industries, to enable them to take their place as healthy competitors in the world markets; and second, a regional policy whose aim will be to maintain the United States as a country in which all geographical areas (and thereby all classes and races) share the burdens as well as the benefits this country has to offer.

The United States must be considered not only as a country but as a continent, and if we are to find remedies for our problems, we must look at half of that continent as a new hybrid: a highly industrialized but nevertheless underdeveloped country that risks becoming poorer, unproductive, ridden with slums. Italy with its Mezzogiorno, France with its southern provinces have attempted to develop the rural areas that lie outside their industrial heartland. We, on the other hand, must maintain both our own crumbling industrial heartland, possibly on a smaller scale, and the urban centers tied to it. It is in the national interest to do so and therefore it is also in the interest of the faster-growing regions.

We need a viable steel industry for our security, not only in the narrow sense that steel is indispensable for weapons but in the larger sense that the United States would be fundamentally weakened if it depended on foreign countries for so crucial a resource. We need a viable auto industry because one out of every eight jobs in this country still depends on it. We need to revive our basic

---

*As I indicated earlier, Chrysler has done infinitely better than I expected. The credit must go to Lee Iacocca, his management, Douglas Fraser and the cooperation of the United Auto Workers. I continue to believe that a Reconstruction Finance Corporation would have provided a sounder long-term approach with an injection of equity rather than debt.

productive industries generally because we need an economy with an effective balance of both manufacturing and services. Our world-wide competitive position requires this from the point of view both of domestic employment and of the balance of payments. We must reduce our requirements for imports and increase as much as we can our industrial self-sufficiency and our ability to export in a decade that will see greater and greater trends toward protectionism as one country after another attempts to solve the payment problems posed by oil imports.

Greater industrial productivity coupled with exports of grain and coal should be the basis for our strategy to offset payments for oil in the 1980s. Moreover, industry has to provide greater employment opportunities for residents of the inner cities. Nothing will do more to erode the confidence of our allies, and consequently our defense positions throughout the world, than the demonstration that we have a nonfunctioning economy with an industrial base in disarray. We need functioning northeastern and midwestern cities because the economic and social costs of their failure will be intolerable.

To redevelop the parts of the United States that are failing, a Reconstruction Finance Corporation should be created for the 1980s.

Would this simply be a renewal of the New Deal? In fact, the original RFC was created by Herbert Hoover in 1918 as part of the post–World War I effort and significantly expanded and activated by Franklin Roosevelt, when it was run by the Texas businessman Jesse Jones. The RFC of the 1930s saved numerous banks, some cities and many businesses, and prevented much larger dislocations from taking place. It financed synthetic rubber development during World War II and new aluminum capacity during the Korean War. It made money for the taxpayer.

The RFC, of course, will be said to interfere with the free-market system. But at present the price of our energy is not freely set; nor is the price of our food; nor the price at which we borrow money. Free markets are clearly desirable, but we do not live in a free-market economy and never will; we live in a mixed economy in which prices and capital are, and will be, subject to government influence.

The RFC should provide the kind of capital our older industries sorely lack: equity capital. In exchange for providing capital to industries that have a sound case for it, and the job security that would come with it, the relevant unions would be asked to make their contributions in the form of wage concessions and changes in work rules that would increase productivity. The lenders, the banks and insurance companies, could be asked to convert some loans to preferred stock and to join with the RFC in committing additional capital. Special classes of securities could be created that would each have appropriate credit ratings and would meet the standards of the "prudent man rule,"* which would make them eligible for purchase by union pension systems. The RFC, like any other large equity investor, should have the right to insist on management changes and changes in the board of directors if it deems them appropriate. It should not become a permanent investor but should act as a revolving fund that can be used to help a given company (or industry) when necessary, and whose holdings can, and should, be sold in the marketplace when it has done its job.

At present, problems like those of Chrysler and New York City can only be dealt with by emergency maneuvers that must take place in front of congressional committees. In the case of New York City, the Municipal Assistance Corporation was able to play a role similar to the one the RFC could play. After its creation as an independent agency by the state legislature, MAC was able to extract concessions from banks and unions, from the city and the state. It was then able to put together a financing package, including federal credit assistance, and to impose fundamental reforms that permitted the city to achieve a truly balanced budget in 1980, five years after near bankruptcy.

The case of Chrysler is an example of how not to proceed. Providing government-guaranteed loans at close to 20 percent interest to a company that has too much debt and no net worth can buy some time, but nothing else. Companies like Chrysler in recent years, and possibly larger ones in the period just ahead, need permanent equity capital in the form of new common stock. Only very large injections of such capital can help make a company's

---

*The "prudent man rule" sets the standards under which fiduciaries such as pension fund trustees are permitted to invest.

survival credible and impel other participants to make the major efforts and sacrifices that have to be made if the company is to be put back into shape. Only an RFC that is publicly accountable but is run outside of politics, like MAC in New York state, could provide such capital as well as negotiate the often stringent concessions that have to come with it. That is beyond the capacity of a congressional committee.

Only now, after over a year of wrestling with the problem, is the Chrysler Loan Guarantee Board beginning to take some of the difficult steps needed to give Chrysler a chance to survive. The board is asking for a total wage freeze (including a freeze on cost-of-living allowances) from the UAW. It is also asking the banks to convert half their loans to preferred stock, and to forgive 70 percent of the balance completely; it is pushing the management to seek a foreign merger or a joint venture partner. The tragedy of this is that it is probably too late and too little. Had these actions been demanded two years ago by an RFC which could simultaneously have promised additional equity capital, it might have had a chance of success. As it was, the congressional committees demanded little and gave a lot. The Loan Guarantee Board, in the middle of a presidential campaign, looked the other way. Now reality is sinking in, but the opportunity has probably been lost. Without substantial fresh capital and a merger partner, Chrysler's chances of survival are minimal. An RFC might have created those possibilities two years ago; it is now probably too late.

Chrysler is hardly an isolated case. A good many large industrial companies, airlines, savings and loan associations and possibly banks could be in serious difficulties if we cannot break out of our current economic miasma of high interest rates, high inflation and low growth and productivity. Some have great hopes for the new Administration's economic program, but there is no guarantee of quick success. Instead of improvising expensive half-measures in the heat of crisis and politics, we should have a safety net to deal with an economic emergency affecting a number of large organizations at the same time.

In each case where a firm sought financing, the RFC staff would have to analyze its chances to survive on a realistic basis, surveying not only conditions in a particular industry but the kind of competition it faced from abroad. The RFC might find that some large firms were beyond help. It might have to insist, as a condition for capital, that the weaker parts of some industries be phased out, that labor contracts be modified, that ways be found to increase productivity. Some firms and unions may find such conditions bitter medicine to take. But it does not seem too much to suggest that, in our current bloated and inefficient economy, the austerities and productivity measures recommended by an RFC could provide a demonstration to other industries of the kinds of reforms that might work for them as well.

An RFC could, at the same time, play a major part in a regional policy. In the Northeast and the Midwest, city after city faces budgetary problems and crumbling infrastructure. The Boston transit system was recently shut down for lack of funds; the New York Metropolitan Transportation Authority (MTA) operates a subway system so old that it poses physical dangers, and the MTA will need $15 billion over ten years to provide adequate service. Bridges and sewers, sanitation and mass transit, schools and firehouses have been allowed to deteriorate. The RFC could provide low-interest, long-term loans to enable municipalities to maintain their physical plants. By improving the quality of city life such investments could help to retain taxpayers while providing jobs to help the existing tax base. As in the case of industrial investments, the RFC could ask for participation by other parties; the various states could be asked to create organizations like MAC to provide local budgetary oversight; the local unions and banks could do their share. As with industry, reform and restructuring would, in many cases, have to be the quid pro quo for receiving capital on favorable terms.

How, might one ask, would such an RFC be set up, capitalized and financed? Congress would have to create a new independent entity with powers to make investments in industries and localities where the RFC deems this in the public interest. Its board of directors could include experienced people from business, finance and labor. An RFC could plausibly begin with capital of $5 billion and authority to issue five times its capital, or $25 billion, in bonds guaranteed by the U.S. government. Its charter should provide that it could not supply more than 50 percent of the financing for any project, the balance to come from the private sector. It could then generate total investment of up to $60 billion. The RFC need not stay in existence more than seven to ten years, after which it could be liquidated, with its assets taken over by the Treasury. Its capital should be subscribed by the Treasury, not necessarily all at once.

The RFC's federally guaranteed bonds could be sold on the open market, but a quite different arrangement seems to me preferable: that they be sold to certain of the OPEC countries with large dollar surpluses, such as Saudi Arabia, Kuwait and the United Arab Emirates. It is time to realize that OPEC is more than an insecure energy source; it is also a more and more important source of capital. At current prices, over the next five years we will pay to OPEC approximately $500 billion for petroleum, about half the present value of all companies listed on the New York Stock Exchange. Possibly a third of that amount, or $150 billion, is likely to be in excess of OPEC's own investment requirements and will consist of short-term dollar balances, most of them belonging to the Saudis, Kuwait and the Emirates, and subject to the whims and winds of Middle Eastern politics.

We must borrow back, on a long-term basis, as much of these funds as possible in order to strengthen the dollar and relieve the pressure on our credit markets. What can we offer in exchange? To the "moderate" oil producers like the Saudis, military protection, continued attempts to find a rational Israeli-Jordanian solution to the West Bank problem and greater efforts at U.S. oil conservation and domestic production to lengthen the life of their reserves. The RFC, with its federal guarantees, would be a wholly appropriate vehicle for investment of these OPEC surpluses, and its use of them would constitute true recycling, in contrast to the present conversion of deposits into short-term paper.

Another possible source of financing would be the surplus funds to be generated by our own oil-producing regions. In Canada, the oil-producing regions have created the Heritage Fund in order to invest several billions of excess dollars in Canadian industry and in the other Canadian provinces. A similar arrangement could be set up here to assist the RFC in its regional policy investments. Why not have Alaska invest some of its excess oil funds in an East

Coast harbor to export coal mined in West Virginia, Ohio and Pennsylvania?*

An RFC by itself could not make an industrial or a regional policy. Tax benefits, changes in federal formulas for welfare and Medicaid, different allocation of defense and synfuel contracts, a coal-based energy plan based in the Northeast and Midwest, temporary measures to protect at least some American industries from foreign competition while they reorganize themselves more efficiently—all these will be required. Temporary protection, however, should always be coupled with needed domestic reform. If the automotive industry is granted a three-year period of restriction of foreign imports, this should be conditional to a three-year commitment to wage restraint on the part of the unions and price restraint on the part of the manufacturers. Similar bargains could be required from the steel industry and its unions, as well as from other industries. The RFC should be the central mechanism, the catalyst.

Of course, none of this is likely to happen tomorrow. The current economic theology—the 1980 version of "laissez faire"—is neither Republican nor Democratic. President Carter's Commission for a National Agenda for the 1980s, a prestigious bipartisan academic group led by William McGill, has just recommended that the government encourage the current population shift to the Sunbelt even though doing so will impose "traumatic consequences" for the major urban centers of the North. The commission argues that we must accept the decline of northeastern and midwestern cities as an inevitable effect of the workings of the market.

This view will not stand up to scrutiny. No doubt there are fundamental difficulties in attempting to halt the shrinkage of metropolitan areas, but it is also true that government policies have heavily contributed to the exodus. We might remind the commission that there were fundamental difficulties in going to the

---

*As I indicated earlier, these proposals for financing an RFC are unrealistic in light of the reduced financial capacity of oil producers, domestic or foreign. However, the Synthetic Fuels Corporation, created under President Carter and presently idle, has some $17–$18 billion of appropriated and expended capital. Part of the capital could readily be used for a new RFC.

moon, in winning World War II, in eliminating slavery. The commission's recommendations epitomize the kind of advice that returned Mr. Carter to Georgia; for it was the perception of him as a President who could not cope with events that defeated him, just as it defeated Herbert Hoover fifty years ago. This country did not become powerful by a mere acceptance of the status quo.

People like the commissioners who throw up their hands at current trends and say "so be it" must be asked to confront the consequences of doing so. In a world where capital will be in shorter supply than energy, is it really a valid use of resources to have to build anew in the Sunbelt the existing schoolhouses, firehouses, transit systems, etc., of the North for the benefit of the new immigrants in the South, instead of maintaining and improving what is already in place? Is it rational to think that northern cities teeming with the unemployed and unemployable will not be permanent wards of the federal government at vast financial and social cost? Shouldn't a commission reporting on our so-called urban problems face up directly to the fact that the future of the cities cannot be discussed separately from the acute difficulties facing the black and Hispanic minorities? Doesn't the notion of "taking the people to the jobs" completely ignore that many of those people, in large parts of this country, are unable and unwilling to move? Is it rational, in the name of the mythical free market, to let our basic industries go down one after the other, in favor of an equally mythical "service society" in which everyone will serve everyone else and no one will be making anything?

Becoming self-sufficient in energy, rebuilding our basic industries and our oldest cities—there is work enough here for everyone in this country as far as the eye can see. Certainly we need tax cuts and regulatory reform and a balanced budget. But alone they will not do the job. Strong presidential leadership working with business and labor will be needed to make these things happen.

In New York City we proved something could be done. In 1975 an activist governor joined with business and labor to keep the city from bankruptcy. We could have simply let the city go, blaming previous mayors, governors, banks, unions; there was also then more than enough blame to go around. The result would have been disaster for the city and great harm to the nation. We chose not to do so. Everyone paid a price: workers with frozen wages and fewer jobs; banks, by providing more and cheaper credit; students, by paying tuition. The riding public was charged higher fares, noteholders had to accept a temporary moratorium on repayment. But today the city, with an equally activist mayor, is thriving economically and has a balanced budget. America cannot survive half rich, half poor, half suburb, half slum. If the country soon wakes up, it will not do so by way of laissez faire; nor will it do so by way of the old liberalism which has proven itself incapable of coping with our present problems. It will do so only by building a mixed economy, geared mostly to business enterprise, in which an active partnership between business, labor and government strikes the kind of bargains—whether on an energy policy, regional policy, or industrial policy—that an advanced Western democracy requires to function, and that, in one form or another, have been made for years in Europe and Japan. This partnership will have to be as indigenous to our culture and traditions as those of Germans and Japanese have been to theirs, and it will have to be competitive. Much is at stake in making such a partnership work. Our ability to protect ourselves and our friends, and to deter our enemies, depends on maintaining a stable, solid economic, industrial and social base at home. Our national security, our industrial power, the strength of our social system itself are all tied to one another and to the need for a new pattern of cooperation to emerge in the United States.

New York Review of Books, March 5, 1981

Chapter Eight

THIS ESSAY WAS WRITTEN DURING THE PRESIDENTIAL
election campaign of 1980 and published in the *New York
Review of Books* in December of that year. As indicated in
other essays, I believed that inflation, oil prices, oil
consumption and interest rates would stay much higher than
they did. However, in the face of world-wide recession the
Federal Reserve relaxed its monetary policies and this,
combined with much reduced loan demand and large inflows of
foreign capital, brought rates down despite staggering deficits.

In this essay I touched on a subject that deserves greater
attention: our relationship with Mexico and Canada. I still
believe that Mexico will be our most important foreign-policy
problem for the foreseeable future. Mexico's staggering debt
and growing population have to be viewed in the context of
our inability to absorb unlimited numbers of immigrants, and
of Mexico's problems with falling oil prices. As of this writing
Mexico appears to be making significant progress toward
economic recovery. However, the downward pressures on
Mexico's standard of living could lead to great social unrest
and potentially radical solutions. Our present concerns with
Central America cannot be resolved without the leadership of
an economically healthy and politically stable Mexico.
Although falling oil prices will be of great benefit to the West
and most of the Third World, we must not delude ourselves
with the notion that our energy problems are solved and that
oil is cheap. Neither is the case.

At the time I wrote this essay, the value of the dollar was

too low; now it is too high. Hence my suggestions for a more orderly international monetary system. I believed that an economic emergency, domestic or international, would face the next President. It happened in the summer of 1982, when the defaults of Mexico and Brazil brought the world banking system close to disaster. The emergency was met by coordinated action by the U.S. Treasury, the Federal Reserve, the International Monetary Fund and the banks. The result was a reprieve, but the danger remains.

I believed then in John F. Kennedy's saying that a rising tide will float all ships. I am much more skeptical today; I suspect a rising tide may float some ships and bypass many others.

I did not anticipate that President Reagan would gain a political victory of sufficient magnitude to pass the radical tax and budget program which the Congress approved in 1981. These tax cuts and defense increases were considerably greater than I expected. Coupled with determined monetarism, they resulted in a recession that was much steeper and a cost in unemployment that was much higher than I expected. Both in the United States and the United Kingdom, inflation came down more rapidly, although at a very high cost.

Although oil prices have come down, we must not overlook the fact that we are still paying out $40 billion to $50 billion annually for imported oil. Large-scale borrowings from OPEC are now impractical, but energy independence is still an objective we should set for ourselves. I believed then, and believe today, that "recycling" is a road to nowhere.

As Chapter 5 indicates, I have become skeptical of tax-based incomes policies or other legislated approaches. I still believe a form of incomes policy is needed to relate prices, wages and productivity, but I now favor a simpler approach to this problem.

I still believe President Carter was on the right track when he tried to form an Economic Recovery Board which, in my judgment, would have led to some version of a Reconstruction

Finance Corporation. Had he put some of these policies into effect earlier, his fortunes (and ours) might have been different.

I am still convinced, as I suggested in this essay, that the United States must speak and act as leader of the Free World. Except in the military domain, our nation is today, at best, an uncertain trumpet.

The Coming Emergency and What Can Be Done About It

DECEMBER 1980

WHAT IS THE OUTLOOK FOR AMERICAN SOCIETY AND, more specifically, how can our society adapt to an economy in distress? It is a vast question that I can only speak to from a rather limited, but nonetheless eye-opening, experience as chairman of New York's Municipal Assistance Corporation. But in brief I would say that the outlook for American society is highly uncertain and that it cannot, in the long run, adapt itself to an economy in distress.

Austerity and democracy do not walk hand in hand in the United States, except in wartime. The near bankruptcy of New York City created in 1975 something like a "moral equivalent of war" for city and state politicians, as well as business and labor leaders. Before then the city had for years been plunging toward disaster. Year-to-year deficits were papered over by accounting gimmicks; pension plans were underfunded; industries were driven away by high taxes and low productivity; borrowing was more and more relied on to finance operating deficits while capital programs were starved; the political leaders refused to face reality: all of these made disaster inevitable.

It was only when this became apparent, when month after month one bankruptcy deadline after another had to be faced, that Governor Carey called on business and labor to join forces with government in order to devise a program that would head off the crisis and bring the city back to life. The programs that accomplished this were initially harshly deflationary, then were followed by a gradual shift to moderately relaxed fiscal policy and support of business, which led this year to New York City's first truly balanced budget in memory.

It is worth analyzing what we were able to do in New York as well as the limits beyond which we could not go, under the severest kind of pressure, since New York is in certain respects a mirror of the United States. There is, after all, little difference between New York City's mounting year-after-year deficits from the mid-1960s to 1975 and the fact that the national budget has been in balance only twice during the last fifteen years; little difference between New York City burying its operating expenditures in its capital budget and the $15 billion annual financing of the United States government that is "off-budget" (i.e., the loan guarantees and similar commitments that do not appear in the budget); little difference between New York City having driven business south and west as a result of high taxes and low productivity and the United States driving business abroad for the same reasons; little difference between New York City selling short-term notes to finance its deficits and the United States financing itself with the shortest of all notes, namely demand deposits of OPEC oil producers; little difference between New York City's skyrocketing pension costs and the requirements that Social Security be adjusted to the cost of living (COLA). New York City faced actual bankruptcy by its inability to pay off its debts when they came due; the United States is facing the national equivalent of bankruptcy in the form of uncontrolled inflation requiring increasing levels of national debt to be paid off in currency worth less and less.

Looking back over the last five years in New York, during which a deficit of $1.8 billion annually was brought to zero with a minimum of social disturbance, one can see two distinct phases. First came the brutal shock of actions intended to stop the hemorrhaging: a wage freeze coupled with deferrals of past increases; a 20 percent reduction in the work force; increases in transit fares; tuition at City University for the first time in 120 years; reduction by the banks of interest rates paid by the city and extension of the time period of the city's loans; shifts in pension costs from the city to the unions; increased taxes; and the creation of a state-run control board to pass on the city's budget.

These programs, most of which were negotiated or set in motion by the Municipal Assistance Corporation, were coupled with limited federal credit assistance. They enabled the state-created MAC to provide a total of $7 billion of long-term financing to the city, both to refinance past accumulated short-term debts and to finance its increasing deficits and increasing capital programs over the period. The large initial layoffs of city employees were followed by a period of limited attrition and then by a stabilization of the work force at its present level; the wage freeze was followed by a two-year labor settlement at an increase of 4 percent annually.

But then austerity had to yield to the reality of society's pressures, and a more recent settlement was made at essentially market rates between management and labor. Tax increases were replaced by tax cuts designed to favor businesses. Harmony was broken by a transit strike this spring. Increasing social tension in the ghettos of Harlem and Bedford-Stuyvesant culminated in ugly demonstrations to block the closing of just one facility of the city's sprawling municipal hospital system. Civil service reform is still politically impossible and real progress on improving management and productivity is largely confined to rhetoric. Some of the city's essential services have deteriorated.

Still, what saved the city was a limited period of austerity, imposed under the direst of threats, followed by gradual relaxation while a prosperous city economy, together with inflation, generated the growth in revenues to bring about a balanced budget. From 1975 to 1980, the expenditures of New York City grew in the aggregate by less than 10 percent, while the state's expenditures grew by 35 percent and the federal government's by 80 percent. The secret of our success, at both the city and state levels, temporary though it may be, was to clamp a lid on expenditure growth while business activity and additional state and federal aid generated enough revenue growth to allow us to survive. As John Kennedy said, a rising tide will float all ships.

It must be remembered that our imposition of extreme austerity was temporary, that it was essentially imposed by outside forces —i.e., the state, the federal government and the workings of the bond market—that it required the courageous political leadership of the governor, as well as a true social contract with business and labor. The people of the city were willing to make real sacrifices as long as they believed that those sacrifices were relatively fairly distributed, that there was an end in sight and that the result would be a better city, a better environment and a better life. What we did in New York City was completely alien to the concepts of "no growth" and the "zero-sum society" so fashionable in economic circles these days.

Americans today are confused and dispirited. They have seen our country, over the last twenty years, dissipate its world-wide economic, military and spiritual leadership at a more rapid rate than any other major power in history. They are accused, with some justification, of being wasteful and lazy by political leaders whom they perceive at best as inept and at worst as corrupt; they hear business leaders calling for belt-tightening and conservative orthodoxy from the comfort of their corporate jets. No wonder people are dispirited.

The United States today, like New York City in 1975, is on the edge of crisis. Financially, militarily, spiritually, we are like an airplane about to stall. The answer, however, does not lie in a simple acceptance of "less for everybody"; I would invite economists of the no-growth school to walk in the South Bronx and convince people there that a reduced standard of living is required to curb inflation. I believe that most Americans would accept, just as New Yorkers did, a limited period of austerity provided they are assured that we are in a crisis that justifies it, they are assured that their particular group is not bearing an unfair share of the burden, and they have a clear sense of how their sacrifice will ultimately lead to a better life for themselves and their children. This requires courageous political leadership with a program that has the following objectives:

- opportunity for private employment for most Americans who want to work
- a strong currency with reduced inflation
- a military policy that will ensure U.S. security against any aggressor

Just as New Yorkers accepted a period of higher taxes, lower services and, in many cases, loss of income for a perceived goal, i.e., the solvency of the city, so now Americans in the rest of the country would, in my view, accept a period of austerity if they really believed there was serious prospect of change. They have no reason to believe that at this point. The presidential campaign has offered little hope in that connection. At this writing it is clear that no matter who is elected, we Americans are condemned, because of uncertain leadership and a Congress unwilling to face responsibility, to stumble from inflation to recession and back, with each stumble worse than the one before. I do not believe that our society will stand the strain over the next four years. Our next President will face an emergency during his term of office, either internationally or domestically, possibly both, and the real issue now is how it will be faced.

It seems to me that we confront different types of critical problems today:

- Problems like that of energy, which should have been apparent for years, where solutions are obvious, but to which the political structure cannot respond.
- Problems of inflation and productivity, about which there is a great deal of theoretical—one might say theological—controversy and very little knowledge, in which the spectrum of professional opinion is exceedingly broad and therefore no political consensus can even begin to be formed.
- Problems of our security vis-à-vis Russia. We do not seem able, at a cost of $140 billion a year, to project a credible sense of the United States as a world-wide power. At the same time, we seem incapable of continuing a process of reduction in weapons competition by ratifying the SALT II treaty.
- Problems like those in the Middle East, which is vital to our security and our economy, where governments tend to be irrational in conduct and far removed from the exercise of our power.
- Problems like employment and education in the ghetto, which have baffled all attempts at improvement and which will, with continued "benign neglect," have consequences that are anything but benign.
- Problems like the great shift in wealth from the Northeast and Midwest to the energy-producing areas of the United States as a result of price decontrol. This trend will ultimately turn the country into "have" and "have-not" regions. One has only to look at Canada for the political implications and to be mindful of the fact that Canada does not have our existing social strains. This is a problem our political leadership resolutely refuses to acknowledge.

- The problem of the West and the Third World, which must be faced by a coherent policy of the Western nations, a willing OPEC and a realistic Third World, none of which exists today. Western technology must combine with OPEC financing to help the Third World. It is beyond the West's capacity to bear any but a small part of the financial costs of Third World development.

- The problem of the coming capital shortage, which will be created by at least three forces: the enormous financing requirements of the United States government; the equally enormous financing that American industry will require to increase productivity and create energy independence; and the drain on our economy of a $100 billion annual payment to OPEC for imported oil. Nonetheless, our economic leaders deny the possibility of a capital shortage.

- The problem of our relations with Mexico and Canada, which pose both large risks and large opportunities for the United States. Mexico, with its oil resources, its fast-growing population and its distrust of the United States, may be our most important long-term foreign policy problem. The potential benefits of a North American Common Market should be explored, but this is not even being discussed peripherally.

These problems are all vital to our future, are all directly related to each other and require inspired political leadership as well as intellectual honesty to find solutions. It is also good to remember that there are no *permanent* solutions to anything, only continuing adjustments to continually changing situations. It seems likely that the current political structure and the existing trends will exacerbate rather than help resolve this series of interrelated problems, and in my judgment this makes a crisis inevitable.

Our energy problem, together with our exposed strategic position in the Middle East, can only be resolved by a strong commitment to practical independence from imports. This would, in addition, strengthen the dollar by eliminating a $100-billion-a-year outflow and would help reduce inflation. A stiff gasoline tax; rational development of coal and nuclear energy with a realistic appreciation of the difficulties with each one; a willingness to compromise on environmental issues—none of these proposals is mysterious or new, and yet current politics makes efforts to explore and implement any of them practically impossible.

Insofar as the economy, inflation and productivity are concerned, we cling to theological explanations that are as tired as they are unworkable. Liberal demands for public works and public jobs have to be matched with the failure of such policies during the past twenty years. But the current conservative proposals for tax cuts that favor production, and for tight monetary policy coupled with tight fiscal policy, have failed with equal consistency. When Presidents Nixon, Ford and Carter tried these methods, they were quite successful in inducing recession, but they wholly failed to reduce inflation; quite the contrary.

The purest attempt so far is in Mrs. Thatcher's United Kingdom, where the teachings of the Anglican Church seem to have been replaced by the "sayings of Milton Friedman." Income tax cuts coupled with sales tax increases, government spending cuts together with tight money, have, after a year and a half, resulted in a 20 percent rate of inflation, an 8 percent reduction in manufacturing output and the highest level of unemployment since the Depression in spite of the enormous cushion provided by England's North Sea oil. In view of the record during the past twenty years, it is relatively easy to understand why liberal economic thinking has become discredited; it is, however, more difficult to understand how the conservative monetarist theology continues to enjoy such uncritical popular support while the current example of England's struggle is vividly in front of us, along with its extraordinary potential for social explosion.

Our business leaders put the blame for inflation on runaway government spending, and call for welfare cutbacks. Government spending is obviously one of several culprits, and putting a limit on welfare and Medicaid spending is a necessity, especially for those of us who live in the Northeast and Midwest. But the only practicable way to limit these programs is to provide private jobs for those on the welfare rolls; it cannot be done without some form of government involvement or subsidy.

We should also, after seven years of experience, be more realistic about the impact of our payments to OPEC. At the current rate of imports, before price rises that inevitably will result from the

Iran-Iraq war, we will, during the next five years, pay over to OPEC approximately half the market value of all companies listed on the New York Stock Exchange. This means that we soon will be turning over the equivalent of half our productive capital built up over the last 200 years for a product we burn every day. Even the lure of huge contracts with the OPEC nations, or the attraction of their large deposits of money in the United States, should not blind us to the economic and political power transferred from the West as well as its inflationary impact. Recycling is a myth; it only means lending more and more to people in Third World countries who can afford it less and less.

We live today in a "padded society" for the majority and a "nowhere society" for millions in the ghettos. It is a "padded society" because everywhere one turns, one finds padding for security: cost-of-living allowances and automatic increases for workers regardless of productivity; constantly increasing unemployment compensation and trade-adjusted payments for laid-off workers; constantly increasing pensions for retirees; every sort of contract and stock options for management regardless of performance; COLAs for recipients of Social Security; government price supports for the farmers.

It is understandable that people want security, but it is the padding of our society that has become our inflationary albatross, not people using credit cards. It is the padding that creates rigidity in wages and prices, regardless of economic activity; that erodes the work ethic; that makes government deficits inevitable in good times and in bad. And management shares guilt with labor and the politicians of both parties by sacrificing the future to avoid facing today. We have created a gigantic pyramid club called "pensions and Social Security" where more and more retired people expect to enjoy higher and higher levels of benefits to be paid by a society producing less and less. While this goes on, in the ghettos of our cities, where there is a 60 percent unemployment rate, young blacks are told to stop pushing drugs and find a job and that welfare is a luxury the country cannot afford.

As in New York City, any national economic program, to have a chance of success, must combine austerity with growth. To begin to control inflation, an incomes policy that relates wage and price increases to productivity is essential. This should be administered through benefits and penalties of the tax system rather than through a new bureaucracy. A freeze of both wages and prices should be imposed until such an incomes policy can take its place. That is one aspect of austerity.

A stiff gasoline tax has to be imposed to permit an overall reduction in interest rates and a strengthening of the dollar. We can have no real growth until our interest rate structure is lowered. This cannot be done responsibly until the dollar is strengthened by other means. Part of the gas tax should finance tax cuts that will lead to increased investment and an increase in military spending. The balance should be rebated to lower-income groups; those in higher-income brackets will just have to pay more. That is another aspect of austerity.

We are in a military competition with the Soviet Union, in which the United States is dangerously deficient in conventional as opposed to nuclear power. Against a standing conscripted army, we try to compete with a volunteer army at immense cost and low effectiveness. We spend $140 billion a year on defense and cannot airlift three divisions into the Middle East. Until the millennium when peace reigns world-wide, we must have an adequate conscripted army with low pay, with no excuses from service except for health and with a highly professional, highly paid cadre of officers and noncoms. That is the third aspect of austerity.

We must rebuild our older cities, as well as our older industries, and we must do so in a way that also brings work to the ghetto areas. I believe this requires the creation of an entity similar to the Reconstruction Finance Corporation of the 1930s and the cooperation of business, labor and government, national and local. Unemployment in the ghetto can be solved either by taking the people to the jobs, which I do not believe to be feasible, or by bringing the jobs to the people. Our older cities, our older industries, our hardcore unemployed are all attached to the same umbilical cord. An independent financing entity is needed to cope with the fundamental restructuring of older industries and the renewal of the physical plant of older cities, and to make use of the work potential of the inner-city unemployed. Providing employment in the private sector to the ghetto dweller is not only a humane social necessity; it is an economic necessity. It cannot be done, however, without cooperation between business and labor and without government support. To the argument that this is undue interference with the free-market mechanism, I would answer that an RFC making equity investments is no different, in basic theory, from a refundable investment tax credit; both methods use taxpayers' money to provide capital to enterprise.

Ultimately this country must look to a future of relatively evenly distributed burdens and benefits, regardless of geography, regardless of class, regardless of race, if it is to maintain itself as a strong democracy. The present trends are in the opposite direction. A determined domestic energy program, coupled with an industrial policy, and the investments in infrastructure and city renewal that go with it, could put the whole country to work for the next twenty years. That, in my view, would be the tide that could float all ships.

Temporary austerity will have to be accepted, on a well-defined basis. We cannot reduce inflation without a tough incomes policy. We cannot limit the growth of government spending without shifting large segments of the population from government support to private employment. This can only happen if there are noninflationary stimuli of the economy, large-scale investment programs, lower business taxes and interest rates, and a strong currency. A stiff gasoline tax to fund part of this program, and a tough incomes policy, together with large-scale long-term borrowings from OPEC, will help protect the dollar and permit the safe lowering of interest rates. An RFC is not state capitalism; it is a temporary mechanism to restructure on a sensible basis those older, basic industries that otherwise will either disappear or be bailed out by indiscriminate government funding.

In addition, the examples of Germany and Japan should convince us that a genuine partnership of business and labor in government is required to accomplish any program dealing with inflation and the economy. I strongly support the Carter Administration's move in that direction with the creation of the Economic Revitalization Board and other similar structures. To cries of elitism or the fear of creating a new "establishment," I say that where we are going otherwise is infinitely worse.

We have recently heard much talk of the Silent Majority, the Moral Majority and other majorities. The fact of the matter is that our country today cannot muster a majority for anything except complaint. The body politic is so splintered and Balkanized that the impotence of the political establishment is a perfectly valid reflection of the negativism and lack of interest of the electorate. A government of checks and balances has become all checks and no balances. As usual, we have heard the presidential candidates orate about cutting government spending and bureaucracy, instituting great programs, changing the country's direction. We all know this will not happen. We must face the reality that our problems are getting larger as the system's ability to cope with them is lessened, a trend that leads over the edge of the cliff. Recently there have been suggestions for fundamental constitutional changes in our government. Some call for a single-term presidency and related limits on congressional terms, others for variations of parliamentary government, as was advocated by Lloyd Cutler in a recent issue of *Foreign Affairs,** or for a congressional cabinet structure.

These do not, however, have serious prospects at present. Only a major crisis will force the kind of constitutional change advocated by serious students of government today. I believe such a crisis is likely to occur because to avoid it, too many things have to go right, all over the world, for too long a period of time. Although it is impossible to predict whether it will be monetary or military, in the Middle East or in Cleveland, the potential for military, economic or social strife is probably too great to be avoided. When a crisis of sufficient magnitude creates the possibility for fundamental change, it will carry with it enough of a popular majority for action so that a President with a real vision of the future will be able to put his program through. That is obviously a risk for democracy as well as a hope.

In the meantime, the best that can be done is to have a government as competent as possible with a coherent program, no matter how difficult to implement. We are for the time being tied into a straitjacket of high inflation, low growth and high unemployment, no matter who the next President may be. This state of affairs carries with it suffering and austerity that are unevenly distributed geographically and socially, and cannot be sustained for very long. It is fantasy, however, to have illusions of real long-term solutions at present.

*"To Form a Government," Fall 1980.

Today we could not build our road system, create the TVA or undertake the Manhattan Project. Between the Congress, the courts and the numerous interest groups, these projects would all die on the vine. The concept of democracy in which the minorities are willing to abide by the will of the majority has been much eroded. What little rationality is left in the system is being eliminated by TV politics in which little capsules of show business are supposed to pass for statesmanship.

This country should be able to speak for the nations and interests of the Western world. To abdicate this role to Helmut Schmidt or Valéry Giscard d'Estaing, no matter how capable they are, is to abdicate our responsibilities. We are, however, in no position to carry our duties out even if we had leaders capable of conceiving what they should be. Whether it be the defense of the Middle East, disarmament negotiations with the Warsaw Pact or the problems of the Third World nations in their fight against poverty and overpopulation, only the United States can provide the counterweight to the mass of China and the shadow of Russia.

In 1939 Neville Chamberlain rose in the House of Commons to speak for the Conservative party when a backbencher yelled: "Speak for England!" The United States, I suggest, should speak for the West. It must speak for opportunity, for growth, for social justice, and it must speak with confidence and power. That will only happen when a majority of Americans decide that the drift has got to stop, and a President with a sense of the future gives direction to the power that will be unleashed. This will not happen today, but it will come sooner than we think.

New York Review of Books, December 4, 1980

Chapter Nine

———— ?❧ ————————————————————————

THIS WAS ONE OF MY FIRST ATTEMPTS TO EXPLAIN the New York City experience to an out-of-state audience. It consists of a speech I gave at the LBJ Library in Austin, Texas, in March 1979.

Jimmy Carter was President of the United States. New York City was well along on the road to recovery, but at the national level, inflation and high oil prices were a considerable threat.

As these essays indicate, I had begun to equate our experience in dealing with New York City's problems with the possibility of dealing with national problems of a similar kind. Looking at this speech in retrospect, I see I may have been somewhat overoptimistic about New York City's ability to maintain reform, although the city's financial condition is now very sound. The Emergency Financial Control Board now exercises its control function quite timidly, and the city's tendency to tax instead of controlling spending is dormant but far from dead.

The ability of business, labor and government to cooperate in New York today is clearly far superior to anything known before the city's fiscal crisis in 1975, and, as a result, New York's performance is far better than that of most American cities. However, a large part of what was achieved, in terms of reform, came in the early years of the crisis (1975–1977), in a period when Governor Carey provided much stronger political leadership to the alliance than in his second term. To be effective, business/labor/government cooperation requires strong and committed political leadership to provide legitimacy and direction.

This essay came after the second oil shock, gas lines and further increases in oil prices. There is, therefore, much emphasis on energy independence, alternative sources and regional initiatives. I still believe these are valid concepts.

Oil prices have come down somewhat, as a result of conservation and recession, but we have not resolved our energy problem. Domestic drilling is dramatically down; synthetic fuels development has died. We will luxuriate in lower gas prices and go back to big cars until the next so-called energy crisis. Then as a result of either economic recovery or supply interruption, or both, we will watch prices rise again.

This essay contains a fairly lengthy description of the Energy Corporation of the Northeast (ENCONO), a regional energy development corporation many of us had great hopes for. It was the product of a regional alliance that had been put together by the northeastern governors and was meant to provide federal assistance to regional efforts in the field of energy. I saw this as a model for other regional structures which, in different parts of the country, would deal with related problems, for example, water. President Carter initially supported the project, but the political leadership from the northeastern governors was weak and the project was finally superseded by the now-defunct Synthetic Fuels Corporation. I strongly believe in the need for regional structures of this kind. The recent grouping of midwestern governors in the Great Lakes Alliance certainly indicates a continuing need for this concept. The reader will recognize readily that my later suggestions for a national Reconstruction Finance Corporation came out of our efforts to create a regional development program. Many of the concepts of ENCONO are maintained in the RFC structure.

I believed then, and I believe today, that businessmen should become more directly involved in public affairs. That is particularly true at the local level, where one can make a tangible and measurable difference, but it can happen only if the political leadership welcomes such cooperation.

Although our rate of inflation has been brought down much more dramatically than I had believed possible, and may fall further as oil prices fall, this relief has come at a very high cost. Many fundamental weaknesses in our economy remain uncorrected. Some have deteriorated further.

At the time of this speech, high inflation and a sharply undervalued dollar were at the top of my list of economic concerns. Today an equally sharply overvalued dollar together with slow growth and deflation in the Third World have taken their place. These oscillations are clearly problems in themselves, and the right answers are somewhere in between. With the benefit of hindsight I would opt for a slightly undervalued dollar instead of a sharply overvalued one.

I have consistently overestimated the likelihood of social unrest in the inner cities. I still believe the risk is there, but I must acknowledge that it has not happened, fortunately.

Looking back on this speech, I see that in common with many businessmen, I tended (and may still tend) toward excessive impatience with the process of public-interest participation in decision-making. Though environmental protection, consumer protection, public safety and clean air and water standards must not be overriden in the name of efficiency, legitimate public interests have to be met within a framework where decision-making is not brought to a complete standstill. When I refer in this speech to cooperation between business, labor and government, I expect the government to be the protector of the public interest and to act in its behalf.

New York Mirrors the United States

IN MAY 1975, NEW YORK CITY WAS HEADED FOR BANK-ruptcy. Government alone was unable to stop the process; at nei-ther the city, state nor federal level could one find the determina-tion, know-how and means to prevent a catastrophe. This was equally true, however, of the business community, especially the financial community, which, having financed the city's excesses, was unable to solve the problem. At stake was the solvency not only of New York City but of the state; an aggregate of over $30 billion in securities could default, then representing approximately 20 percent of the capital of the U.S. banking system. The implica-tions of such a mammoth bankruptcy went beyond our own econ-omy and could have severely threatened the dollar, and with it the international monetary system.

Federal officials who had no solutions pretended there was no major problem; local officials pretended the problems would go away if the banks would only provide credit; the banks, having lent too much, said enough is enough.

At that point Governor Carey approached the business commu-nity and it, in turn, joined hands with labor. New structures came into being, structures that represented the combined forces of government and the private sector. The Municipal Assistance Cor-poration (MAC) was created to finance the city; the Emergency Financial Control Board (EFCB) was created to bring the budget into balance. In the case of MAC, a state agency, with a board of directors consisting solely of private citizens appointed by the governor, was given control over $1.25 billion of annual tax reve-nues against which it could issue bonds; in the case of the EFCB, a board consisting of four public officials—the governor, the mayor and two controllers—and three private citizens was given the power of approval over the city's budget. Since then, MAC has provided the city with over $10 billion of financing on its own and spearheaded the city's efforts to obtain federal guarantees for another $1.65 billion; the EFCB has provided the pressure to bring the city's budgetary deficit down from $2.5 billion to about half a billion dollars currently, with final balance expected within three years.

MAC and EFCB were instrumental in such unpopular but necessary decisions as the institution of tuition at City University, a 30 percent increase in transit fares, a wage freeze and wage deferral program with the city unions, a 20 percent reduction in the work force with new emphasis on productivity, and long before Proposition 13 became fashionable, a tax cap followed by downward pressure on property tax rates.

We have not solved all of our problems in New York City, far from it, but in a finite period of time, a runaway, seemingly intractable problem of vast dimensions was brought under control. More important, the direction and philosophy of a large unit of government were fundamentally and permanently changed as a result of the involvement (some would say intrusion) of the private sector in government. In my judgment, this is a principle that is applicable to many national problems. It is this conviction that led me to accept with great pleasure the opportunity of addressing this symposium.

The United States today is similar in many ways to New York City in 1975; loss of private sector jobs, year-after-year deficits, lowered productivity, higher and higher taxes, reliance on short-term debt to avoid facing tough issues, hidden liabilities in the form of unfunded pensions and Social Security—all of these sound terribly familiar to those of us who wrestled with similar tendencies in New York City. What is the difference, after all, between the refusal of the Republic National Bank in Dallas to buy New York City notes and the reluctance of the Swiss Bank Corporation to hold U.S. dollars? Both are making judgments not only about the soundness of the credit but about the underlying strength of the economic unit and, equally important, about the effectiveness of its political leadership.

The involvement of private citizens in the affairs of New York City, in partnership with government officials, clearly avoided a potential disaster that neither the private sector nor government alone was capable of solving. One has only to look at the problems of Cleveland to see what can happen when such a partnership fails to jell. Cleveland went into default, and may yet sink into bankruptcy and chaos, because the mayor and the business community were at loggerheads. Luckily for us, Cleveland's default, involving some $15 million, is irrelevant from a financial point of view. But for the people who live there it can turn out to be catastrophic. It is also a political disgrace. There was no need for Cleveland to go into default; the means were there to prevent it and the talent was there to find alternatives. It happened because there was no will, no dialogue, no structure that encompassed, under one roof, local government and the private sector.

In referring to the private sector, I hasten to include labor as well as business. The steps taken to save New York City required legislative action, both in Albany and Washington, as well as massive financing. Without the political support of the municipal unions neither MAC nor the EFCB could have come into being; the opposition of local politicians would have been too great. Over the last four years union pension systems acquired several billion dollars' worth of our bonds, but at least as great a contribution was their political support at the local and national levels.

In addition, what may be the most important structure of all came into being almost by chance. After a particularly virulent clash between the city, the unions and the banks, communications broke down. Walter Wriston, chairman of Citibank, Jack Bigel, representing the unions, and I began talks that resulted in an informal grouping with the quaint acronym of MUFL (municipal unions/financial leaders). At regular intervals the members of this group, consisting of the heads of the clearinghouse banks, the leaders of the unions and the chairman of MAC, take joint positions in areas where they can agree. Welfare reform and tax reductions for business were but two examples. If you don't think that municipal labor supporting high-bracket tax reduction in Albany is revolutionary, think again. Equally significant is the fact that we discuss everything of importance to the city and state, including areas where the unions and banks cannot possibly agree institutionally. City and state officials, occasionally including the mayor and the governor, regularly attend and participate in these sessions. The importance of this exercise is in the area of mutual understanding. Tensions, at times of crisis, between these financial and political power centers have been considerably reduced. Personal relationships of respect and understanding have been created where previously suspicion and mistrust turned every problem into a confrontation. The lowered decibels in the public arena permitted political accommodation without loss of face, an impossibility a few years ago.

Four years ago, when Governor Carey drafted me in our fight against bankruptcy, I had literally never met a city or state official, a local union leader or a newspaper editor. I was a complete virgin, municipally speaking. Today that virginity has been lost, but, like all erstwhile virgins, I have learned a lot: about government, local and national; about labor; about politics; and about the media. This experience, which I would not have missed for anything in the world, nonetheless causes me deep concern about the ability of our governmental institutions alone to cope with our problems; skepticism about the ability of our political system to survive if those problems are not faced; and a conviction that solutions, if any, can come about only in cooperation between government and the private sector and in structures that combine the best of both.

Democracy is, without any question, the noblest as well as the most agreeable form of government ever invented. It may, however, be a luxury that requires an abundance of resources, and these resources may be on the point of running out. It is worth considering, at a time when expectations have been raised everywhere in the world, whether democracy could survive an extended period of austerity and reduced standard of living, except in wartime. And yet, with many of our governmental institutions paralyzed or inept, with overregulation and bureaucracy stifling the basic entrepreneurial drive of business, austerity is where we are headed if we are lucky—much worse if we are not.

What are some of the major danger areas at this point and why would business/government partnership help? First and foremost is probably energy. In one of the most pathetic examples of political impotence and national lack of will, the United States, following the clear warning of the oil embargo of 1973, is more dependent on imported energy than ever. We cannot afford major supply interruptions without an industrial crisis; we cannot afford major price increases without a financial crisis; we cannot maintain the status quo without letting our banking system become hostage to OPEC. An all-out domestic energy production program, in addition to stringent conservation measures, is an absolute necessity. It will require gradual oil and gas price deregulation as well as new institutions to speed the process along. A national energy development bank or, alternatively, a series of regional development banks should be created to deal with projects too large or risky for the private sector alone to undertake. They should have powers of expediting the process of siting, permits, state-by-state differentials, and so forth.

In the Northeast we have been working on such a project for three years and are about to reintroduce legislation to begin it in the U.S. Senate. ENCONO, the Energy Corporation of the Northeast, will have equity capital of $1 billion owned by the seven northeastern states on a formula based on population. The corporation will have the right to issue $15 billion in bonds to be guaranteed by the U.S. government. It will be managed by a board of directors of private citizens appointed by the governors and run by professionals hired by the board. It will operate in partnership with private companies and is not permitted to own or finance more than 50 percent of any project it is involved in. It will have the power to expedite projects and, through its relationship with the governors and the states, will have considerable political leverage. It should be the catalyst for projects too large or risky to be undertaken by the private sector alone and will turn over its portfolio of investments to the private markets as projects become commercially viable.

Our cost of energy in the Northeast is two and a half times the average of the rest of the country, since we are so dependent on imported crude oil. However, lowering that cost by switching to domestic production will help the fight against inflation, help the fight to protect the dollar, and create jobs and revenues. In addition, if this project gets congressional approval, we should attempt to interest some of the OPEC countries in purchasing ENCONO's federally guaranteed bonds, thus recycling petrodollars on a long-term basis with a project that would lengthen the life of their own reserves.

Creating the concept of ENCONO, bringing it along to this

stage and running it when launched are all products of business/ government cooperation. Having seven states agree on anything is miraculous. In this case, seven states agreed on a concept by having each governor appoint one person from the private sector and one person from his own staff as his representatives. This group of fourteen then developed the concept over a period of several months and reported back to the Coalition of Northeast Governors (CONEG), their principals. CONEG blessed it, staffed it legislatively and administratively, and a bill was introduced last year, sponsored by all the senators of the region. I had the privilege of acting as Governor Carey's private representative on ENCONO, which is, like MAC, a classic example of business/government cooperation. The concept came about in partnership, away from the political hurly-burly; the corporation itself will be run like a private business but will be publicly accountable because of gubernatorial appointments and Treasury oversight. In ENCONO's progress in the Congress, I expect that our business leadership as well as our labor leadership will actively support it.

The concept of regional development banks combining private management with public funding and accountability seems to me applicable in areas other than energy, depending on a particular region's problems. Western water problems, southern rural industrialization problems, northeastern and midwestern energy problems can be attacked more vigorously and effectively in this fashion.

The tasks facing this country are monumental. But tackling them vigorously would provide the jobs and the revenues that will be needed if the social infrastructure is to be maintained. In addition to an energy program aimed at making us relatively self-sufficient, we need a railroad system that is viable. We need a steel industry that is competitive. We need to bring private employment to the inner-city ghetto, which is becoming a social time-bomb. We need clean air and rivers. None of these programs can even be conceived without business/government partnership or—more to the point—business/government/labor partnership.

A different area in which business/government partnership can pay big dividends is rather far removed from actual day-to-day operations. It consists in helping to create a public climate that permits political leaders to make unpopular decisions without committing hara-kiri.

Again I look back on our experience in New York City. As much as anything else, the influence that the private members of MAC and the EFCB exerted was on the political process itself. This was due to the public support we gained as a result of a supportive press. Early on we made a fundamental decision to be totally candid with the press. It was a decision that entailed risk since we were continuously teetering on the brink of bankruptcy. The press, however, once it understood what we were trying to do and why, treated us with fairness, supported us and created the climate in which political leaders could do difficult and painful things. Tuition at City University, transit fare increases, service reduction—the entire budget-balancing process consisted of one unpopular decision after another. However, not only could politicians do difficult things, but those things also turned out to be good politics. Governor Carey's popularity never stood so high as after that long summer of 1975, when together with us he led the fight against bankruptcy.

Business/government cooperation already exists on a large scale at the local government level. New York's case may have been extreme, brought on by an emergency, when private citizens actually participated to a considerable extent in the governmental process. In many other cases the cooperation is less formalized but nonetheless effective. Businessmen, after all, provide jobs, capital spending and so on. The political sector is more and more in need of increased revenues without increased taxes, and business activity is the best answer.

For the cooperation to be as effective as possible and for it to function at the national level rather than simply at the local level, businessmen will have to make efforts of their own and undertake certain risks. By and large, businessmen have been ready and willing to *serve* government as opposed to working *with* government. As cabinet members and commission chairmen, presidential advisers and ambassadors, they have served the country well. They are usually timid, however, about getting involved in "politics" and, through the media, in taking public positions on a variety of issues. It is an understandable timidity. Politics is probably the cruelest form of activity known to man, short of cannibalism. Not as cruel but equally risky is the involvement with the media. There is always the possibility of embarrassment, of making people angry and attracting fire from various quarters. There is the possibly greater danger of getting hooked on being a public figure, of believing that your own inane statement because you read it in the New York *Times* is all of a sudden imbued with wisdom. However, if businessmen are to play the role they can and should play in a world increasingly in need, they will have to come into the real world and deal with politics and the press.

Labor leaders, far better than businessmen, understood long ago that involvement in public affairs and a direct relationship with the media were powerful instruments to get political attention. The business leader who wishes to make an impact has to do the same thing. His views may have the wisdom of Solomon; if they have the editorial support of the *Times* and the *News* they will become public policy.

Increasingly today the problems of government are two-fold: first, political impotence; second, bureaucratic ineptness. Business-government cooperation can help in both areas.

Political impotence is the result, in great measure, of the paralysis caused by splinter groups exercising veto power at every level of government. The concept of democracy has been distorted to permit the will of various minorities, through manipulation of the legislative as well as the judicial process, to turn what should be a review process into veto by endless delay. If that were not enough, excessive regulation, coupled with the ordinary amount of bureaucratic ineptness, has added layer upon layer of cost to an economy already struggling to contain inflation and remain internationally competitive. A change in political climate is needed to cope with such paralysis. Involved businessmen, in partnership with labor, can have an impact at the grassroots level and provide political leaders with a platform for action.

Increasingly, as we face the possibility of a serious economic downturn as well as runaway inflation, the creation of jobs and the maintenance of purchasing power will be the issues of the day. Most businessmen understand that there is more to business than just profits—that there is also the moral imperative of affirmative action, social responsibility, environmental protection—but all of this must occur within the framework of an ongoing economic and social unit and with the understanding that, for the businessman and his company, tomorrow always comes. The businessman, if he has credibility and is willing to take the risks, can be of enormous help to political leaders. In New York state, a council of business and labor leaders, which I have the privilege of chairing, has just been appointed by the governor to try to untie the straitjacket in which many of our more significant economic development projects find themselves. Whether they are new power plants, industrial parks or a convention center, they need an enormous push. Our council intends to do just that.

With respect to solving the problem of bureaucratic incompetence, business can contribute by participating in the creation and management of new, mixed public/private structures which are bound to come into being. Whether in local structures like MAC and the EFCB, regional structures like ENCONO or national structures of a similar nature, business and government can circumvent bureaucracy as well as take certain well-defined tasks out of the political tug-of-war that government agencies are subject to.

Jean Monnet's European Coal and Steel Authority and the European Atomic Energy Community were the kind of structures in which government and business joined hands for a specific task. Their impact, however, went far beyond the task itself and resulted in new perceptions and understanding which brought forth the European Common Market and are right now bringing forth a European Currency Union.

The suggestion that government and business join hands in new structures invariably brings the cry of socialism and New Dealism from the right and charges of corporatism from the left. I must confess, in the interest of full disclosure, that I grew up as a New Deal liberal. When I came to this country as a refugee during World War II, Franklin Roosevelt was my hero, the New Deal an unparalleled intellectual achievement. I believed in government's ability to manage, to right wrongs and make things work. I was also, obviously, totally ignorant of government and its functioning. Today I am neither liberal nor conservative, but profoundly skeptical. The fact that I find government, at any level, neither inspiring nor efficient does not, however, lead me to conclude that we can or should do away with it. It leads me to the conclusion that as citizens we must encourage and inspire our government and help it toward greater efficiency.

We live with primitive economic slogans today, most of which cannot stand the test of reason. They are partly the result of TV newscasting, which turns complex problems into two minutes with Walter Cronkite. They are the result of public officials selling themselves to the voters with thirty-second commercials on the same news programs. Some of these slogans have become conventional wisdom, and some of this wisdom seems to me nonsense. The concept of a "service economy," for instance, strikes me as simply a cop-out. It merely says: "These are the current tides and there is nothing we can do about them."

These are indeed the current tides, but there is much we should do about them. I believe that no industrially developed society can function for long unless the main part of its economic activity comes from the production of goods. The "service economy" concept is justified by the "free trade" religion. But is it really in this country's interest to run up tens of billions of dollars of balance-of-trade deficits with Japan, destroy the value of our dollar and decimate some of our manufacturing industries? I think this is an arguable proposition.

In keeping with our tendency to reduce complex issues to simple slogans, today's political and economic philosophies seem to oscillate between two equally unsatisfactory schools of thought: 1) the neo-conservative thesis that "government is inept, therefore the less government does, the better it is"; and 2) the liberal thesis that "we can afford anything as long as we can print money." The former is intellectual bankruptcy; slicing the salami ever thinner will not solve the problems of a country of a quarter of a billion people with a rapidly growing permanent underclass. The latter will lead to actual bankruptcy, in the form of runaway inflation, which we are approaching by leaps and bounds as it is.

We must be able to come up with answers other than a constitutional convention for a balanced budget, a 30 percent across-the-board tax cut or national health insurance. If we really want a constitutional convention to stop inflation, let us provide that no elected official can run for reelection when the consumer price index rises more than 6 percent annually. That would get my vote. In the meantime, however, we have to be more active, innovative and aggressive in dealing with energy, productivity, exports, inflation. We have to link the legitimacy of government with what is left of entrepreneurship if we are to maintain our political system.

We in New York City created the equivalent of a coalition government to manage an austerity program—a coalition of government, business and labor. And it worked. A similar coalition must be created at the national level if we are to show the rest of the world that our system really works where it should: at home.

There are risks, of course, in any course of action, but the risk of inaction today is clearly greater. Action carries with it the risk of failure, which is hateful. But to fail without trying is despicable. The concept of partnership carries risks both for government and for businessmen, but the risks must be taken. The destinies of countries were never shaped by fatalists.

Address before symposium on government and business,
Lyndon Baines Johnson Library, Austin, Texas,
March 1, 1979

Chapter Ten

I DELIVERED THIS ADDRESS HALFWAY THROUGH THE Carter presidency. I had just visited Israel for the first time, and had been exhilarated by the spirit of its people. At the same time, I was becoming more and more concerned with the apparent lack of commitment of the American people, symbolized by the low turnouts of voters in elections. Hence, this short speech.

Although the direction of national policy has changed sharply since the election of President Reagan, the basic questions that I raised in this speech remain unanswered. The recent sharp increase in black and Hispanic voter registration may be a new element in our political life and could have significant repercussions. The possibility of a "national" government, to include the best minds in this country, regardless of party affiliation, strikes me as an idea whose time is coming.

Today Israel is divided by many issues similar to those that have haunted America. The invasion of Lebanon created, for the first time, a profound internal division over the justice of a war. The annexation of the West Bank territories is raising equally disturbing questions within Israel as to the moral direction the country is taking. And racial tensions between Sephardic and Ashkenazy Jews strike a melancholy note that we know only too well.

I would not make this speech today using Israel as an example. The security of Israel is all-important to me, but so is the survival of her soul. Israel cannot be blamed for not making peace when, aside from Egypt, all of her neighbors wish for her destruction. But I still yearn to think of her as Athens instead of Sparta. Events may not make it possible.

Commitment

THE HOLIDAY SEASON IS IN FULL SWING. THANKSGIVING is over, election day is behind us, Christmas is around the corner; everybody feels optimistic. We have much to be thankful for. New York has survived. Peace may come to the Middle East. The economy is still strong.

But we live in unusual, confusing times, and bizarre things are happening. Washington tries to save the dollar by selling our gold, and to control inflation by a guaranteed-to-be-mild recession. We will try to balance the budget while we increase defense spending by cutting back our spending on the poor and the cities, even though the decay of urban America could be more dangerous than Soviet ambitions. We begin our negotiations with the oil-producing countries, which have already bankrupted the Western world, with the proposition that a further 7 percent price increase would be modest and would make up for the erosion of the dollar which the oil producers have already helped erode in the first place. A theological argument takes place among economists (who, like dermatologists, never seem to solve anybody's problems, but always travel first-class) as to whether we are headed for a mild recession, or a rolling readjustment, or stagflation, or anything that doesn't sound serious and frighten anybody. Howard Jarvis, whose Proposition 13 is as effective a method for dealing with our problems as a neurosurgeon operating with a meat-axe, is acclaimed in Washington as a modern Moses down from the mountain. Just as in the 1960s all truth and wisdom were supposed to reside in that segment of our population barely beyond the age of puberty, so today wisdom comes to us from self-styled conservatives whose economic notions are out of *Alice in Wonderland.* If all of this seems a little strange, it should not be surprising when we look at how we elect our government, and how our leaders, once elected, then govern.

In the last election almost two out of three people of voting age did not exercise their franchise, while the 37 percent of the people who voted were sold candidates the way Procter & Gamble sells detergent. During news programs and football games, *The Mary Tyler Moore Show* and Monday night movies, we were bombarded with thirty-second spots that turned each candidate into an actor. With opinion polls telling the candidates what the voters wanted to hear, and ample money to make sure the voters heard it over and over again, men and women who, with few exceptions, follow rather than lead were given power by a minority of the electorate. Once in office, the same process continues; if saying what the polls tell you to say gets you elected, why not do what the polls tell you to do to stay in office? The trouble is that polls cannot teach you to lead in a crisis; in 1939 when a backbencher screamed at Neville Chamberlain, "Speak for England," he wasn't asking him to take a poll, he was asking him to lead.

Today, despite our current prosperity, we face dangers and uncertainties ahead, fully as deadly as those England faced in 1939. Our economy is out of control, our currency is in danger, our institutions of government unresponsive or inept. The interaction, at every level, between the executive and legislative branches of government produces fewer and fewer solutions to greater and greater problems. We are engaged in a world-wide competition with a brutal, totalitarian ideology, but whether we win or lose depends on whether we can show that our system works, and not on the size of our cruise missiles or the killing range of the neutron bomb. This means not only controlling inflation for the housewife in Columbus but providing education and employment for the young black in Harlem, and providing a hard dollar for the gnome in Zurich.

We are, by any standard, the richest country in the world. We carry the heritage of democracy handed down from Pericles through the great figures of French enlightenment to our founding fathers. Yet we treat this heritage, the most precious of our possessions, with contempt when we abdicate our responsibility to vote, contempt in the way we manage our affairs, contempt in our acceptance of mediocre leadership.

I traveled recently to Israel for the first time. From a jumble of impressions, one came through most strongly: commitment. Commitment to freedom, commitment to survival, commitment to a way of life. People from all backgrounds, from all over the world, clawed a country out of rock and desert, fought for it against great odds, prevailed, and fight to keep it every day. We, on the other hand, with more to fight for than anyone else, seem unwilling to make the slightest effort. Commitment is not fashionable. Cool is the order of the day. Today men with blood as thin as water flaunt their passions as cold as ice. But Pericles was not cool—neither was Thomas Jefferson, nor Winston Churchill, and they made and preserved our world.

Commitment is not a museum piece. A great Frenchman, Jean Monnet, changed the face of postwar Europe when, through sheer personal willpower, he brought about first the European Coal and Steel Authority and then the European Common Market.

Commitment saved New York City from a bankruptcy that many cool and sophisticated people precipitated. New York survived because some of its committed citizens would not let it fail, because these New Yorkers willed it not to. At a time of visible, palpable crisis, people rallied around: private citizens and politicians, Democrats and Republicans, union leaders and bankers, first with a program to stem the tide, second with a program to rebuild the foundation, third with a program for recovery. Recovery may still be a long way off, but we have stemmed the tide and rebuilt the foundation.

America's strength can be enormous—moral, economic, military. In the last twenty years, peaceful revolutions have transformed our society: civil rights and human rights, the emergence of women as an economic and political force, the concern for the environment. Our economy recovered from the last recession and is still going strong. But underneath it all, there are weaknesses, economic and social, which, if not contained, will sap our strength.

The situation of America today is not so different from that of New York City in 1975. The similarities are striking:

- increasing deficits, internal and external, year after year, papered over with accounting gimmicks to allow politicians to sidestep politically difficult decisions

- increasing reliance on borrowed money to finance those deficits (New York financed itself with short-term notes; the United States does it with borrowed Arab oil money) while neglecting capital formation, with resulting dramatic deterioration of physical plant
- creating greater and greater hidden liabilities in the form of unfunded private and public pensions, Social Security, etc.
- losing private-sector jobs, driven out by high taxes and low productivity
- continuing to absorb large numbers of illegal immigrants at a time of high unemployment

New York City was required to prepare a comprehensive multi-year program to cope with our crisis. We had the good fortune to have a governor willing to put his neck on the line and provide leadership, since the program demanded sacrifice from everyone —a reduced labor force, a stretched-out debt, higher transit fares, City University tuition, some rolled-back pension costs and temporarily increased taxes. Our future in New York is still bleak because the country's future is unclear, but we averted a catastrophe because, in a time of need, we were able to act together, we were able to commit, and leadership lived up to our commitment.

What the country faces is not a bigger or smaller recession, more or less inflation, a stronger or weaker dollar. Those are all effects; they are not causes. We face the possible loss of our most precious asset, democracy, surely the most magnificent form of organized life, because we are lazy, cynical and unwilling to make the effort, unwilling to demand the kind of leadership democracy requires. It is easy to blame the politicians, but we put them in office by our votes or our failure to vote. It is easy to blame the unions, but we in the business leadership have exercised no greater restraint. It is easy to blame the press, the academicians, almost anybody but ourselves.

We are at war today: with inflation, with unemployment, with lack of education, with racial discrimination. We are, furthermore, not winning. If we lose, our system of government may not survive. Whether we wind up with left-wing or right-wing authoritarianism is irrelevant; poison is as lethal served from the left as from the right.

New York City found itself at war and put in motion the equivalent of a wartime austerity program and coalition government. A coalition government should manage a similar program on a national scale. If this means gas rationing in order to reduce oil imports, so be it; if it means wage and price restraints, voluntary or mandatory, for some time, so be it; if it means temporarily limiting imports from Japan, so be it.

The President must mobilize the country's dreams as well as its muscle and demand that the people and the Congress support a true wartime program. The hour is very late, almost as late for the United States as it was for New York in 1975. In the city we fought against bankruptcy; Washington is now fighting the same thing but calls it controlling inflation, protecting the dollar, avoiding a recession.

The real question is whether a democracy can find leadership, nobility of purpose and sacrifice only in a time of crisis, at the brink of disaster. Or can it face up to its problems in times that appear to be normal, when the crisis is still only dimly perceived on the horizon? We will soon have the answer, but if the President loses this fight—if collectively we cannot create the climate to help him win—the result will not be a moratorium imposed upon our noteholders or a wage freeze imposed on the unions, but possibly the end of a form of government that since the days of the French Revolution has done more for more people than any other system ever invented. There will be no winners or losers then, simply the story of another nation that was unable to count its blessings and lost sight of its values.

Address before the French-American Chamber of Commerce,
New York City, December 1, 1978

Afterword

———— ⧟ ————————————————————————

AT THE TIME OF THIS WRITING OUR ECONOMY LOOKS
robust, although it is obvious that major problems remain as a
result of our budgetary deficits, the level of our national debt,
the strength of the dollar and the financial situation of the
Third World. Abroad, things are looking bleak. The Middle
East looks increasingly unstable, Latin America is in ferment,
the Soviet Union and the United States appear utterly
unwilling or unable to stop a nuclear arms race now totally out
of control. Looking at the world at large, it is hard to know
whether the population bomb in the so-called less developed
world, the atom bomb in the so-called developed world, or the
debt bomb in the financial world is the greatest danger; what is
certain is that not much is being done to defuse any one of
them.

At home, dazzling and explosive technological advances in
electronics, communication, pharmaceuticals and genetics,
space travel and exploration, and many other areas point to a
future of hope and progress. At the same time, inner-city
ghettos, black unemployment, inadequate education and
increasing inequality between classes, races and regions will
surely prevent us from achieving such a future unless they are
dealt with and corrected.

This collection of essays is not meant to be a political
document, although it may be interpreted as such. I am a
Democrat by registration as well as by inclination. When I
came to this country in 1942, FDR represented America to me
and stood for the kind of government philosophy I still believe

in today. It goes without saying that this philosophy has to be adapted to the times and to the means at hand. I have, nevertheless, not attempted to write a "Democratic manifesto"; it would be presumptuous on my part to try. I consider myself an "independent" Democrat. I have found in my work for New York City and New York state many Republicans who share my general views and philosophy, in the city and state legislatures as well as in the U.S. Congress. I have supported, and will continue to support, many of them for public office.

In a world of labels, my label is clearly more "liberal" than "conservative." But in analyzing the meaning of this label, a brief look at the record is warranted. New York City has a balanced budget, practically no short-term debt and full access to the financial markets. Management/labor relations are cooperative and economic development is a high priority. The mayor, the governor and many others deserve the lion's share of the credit; as chairman of MAC for the last eight years I have had the privilege to be very much involved in the process. That is my brand of liberalism.

I was extremely hesitant to put in book form what is only a series of essays and speeches, written over an extended period of time, with the infirmities inevitably connected with such an endeavor. What finally prompted me to do so was a desire to stimulate debate on what these essays concern. It is not important to me whether, ultimately, the issues raised herein are dealt with along the lines I suggest, or in totally different ways; what is important is that they be dealt with. That is the purpose of this book.

About the Author

FELIX G. ROHATYN was born in Vienna and came to America with his family in 1942. He graduated from Middlebury College and then began working at Lazard Frères, the New York investment banking firm, of which he is now a partner. He has been the chairman of the Municipal Assistance Corporation (MAC) since 1975, when he was instrumental in saving New York City from bankruptcy. He lives with his wife, Elizabeth, in New York.